ia Breeze

and Steve Bass...

Wakes me up in the mornin'

Rocks me to sleep at night

I've got a red bird singin' on my window sill

I know everything will be all right

Livin' in the Sweet Virginia Breeze

Just sittin on my back porch

I'm just watchin' the sun come up

Sweet sweet Virginia Breeze

blowin' ripples 'cross my coffee cup

Because he must've been thinkin' bout me when he planted

that very first dogwood tree

cause when that breeze comes blowin' through the trees

you know everything will be alright

Livin' in a Sweet Virginia Breeze

Sweet Virginia Breeze

WCVE Public Radio

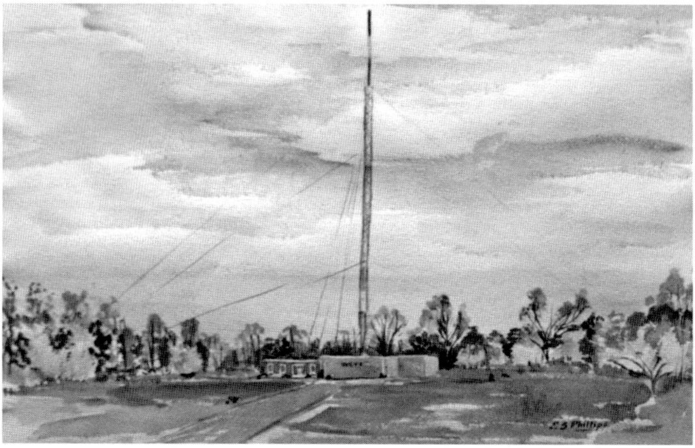

The Community Idea Stations are very pleased to be a part of *The Songlines of Richmond.* Over the years, we have had the privilege of partnering with a number of outstanding arts and cultural organizations to allow people throughout the area to experience music and performances that are comforting, entertaining, and inspiring. In addition to our local efforts, we are pleased to open the doors to concert halls and other venues all around the world.

We have always subscribed to the belief that economic and personal vitality is more likely to exist in a community where support for arts and culture is vibrant and strong. We all have an inherent need to experience and express life in a variety of ways. That's why we value our many partnerships with local organizations like the Richmond Symphony and why we have been so pleased to support events like the Richmond Folk Festival. Any time we can help provide an expanded forum for local artists and local performers to share their creativity and talent, we believe that we have the potential to make a positive contribution.

This book captures some of the best memories and tells some of the best stories about this important aspect of our community. I have no doubt that readers will find something that peaks their interest or allows them to expand their horizons.

It is our great pleasure to be a partner in this endeavor.

A. Curtis Monk, President & CEO, Community Idea Stations

The Songlines of Richmond

A Celebration of Performing Arts, Artists and Stages

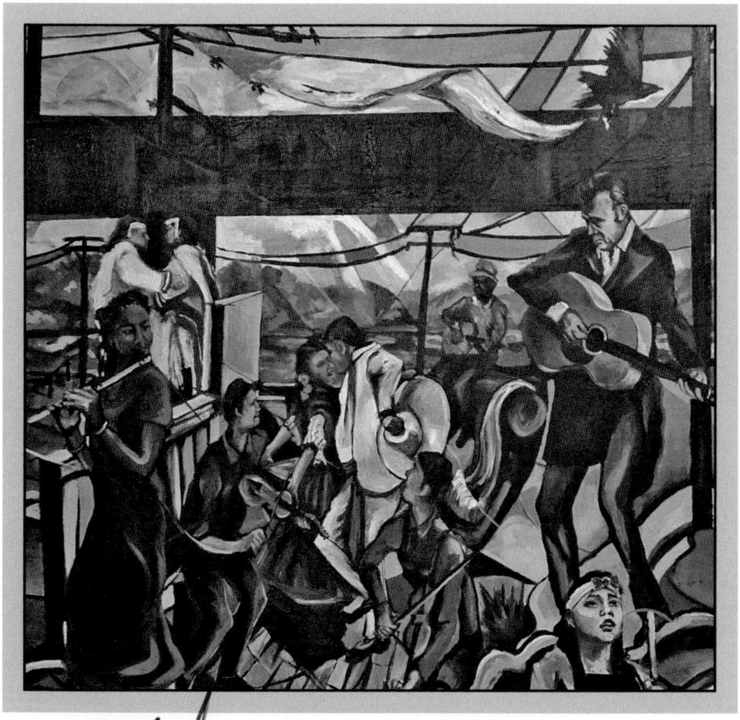

CO-AUTHORS

Brooks Smith & Wayne Dementi

FOREWORD BY

JIMMY DEAN

DEDICATION

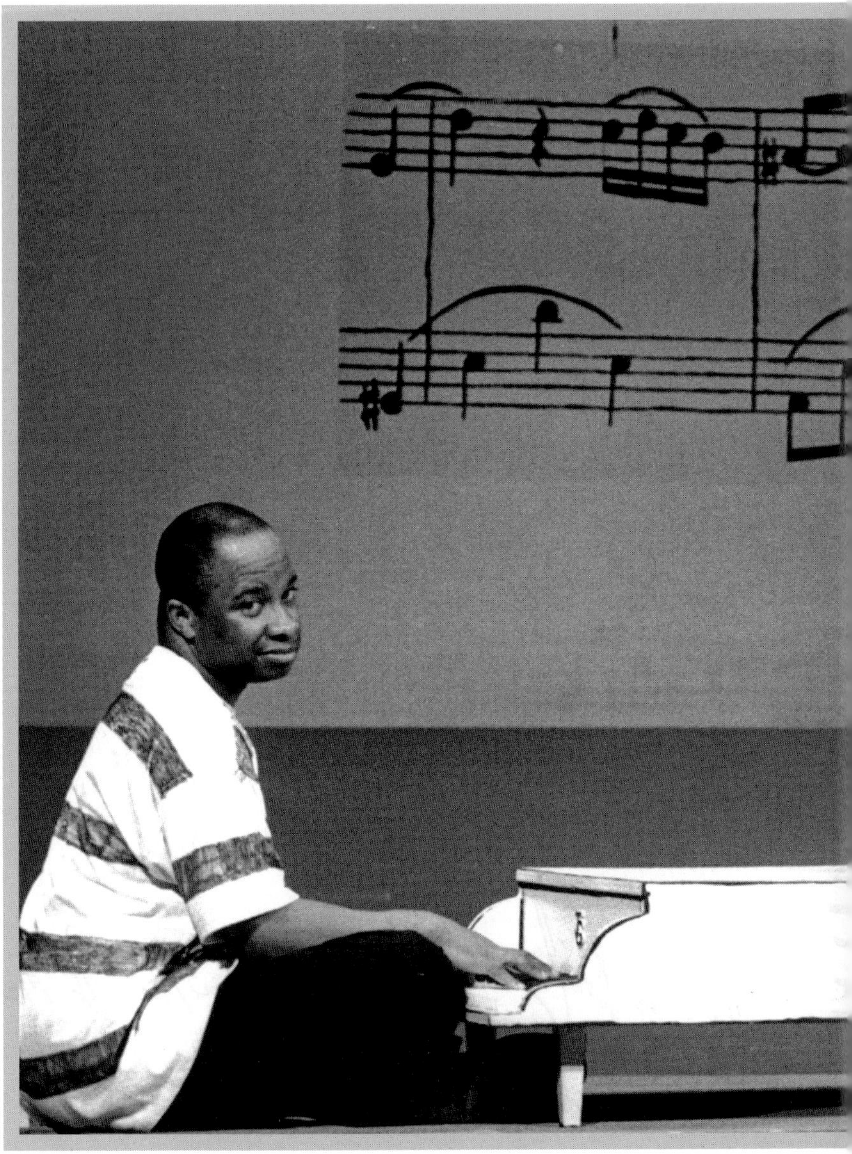

This book is dedicated to anyone who has ever tapped a toe, dippe

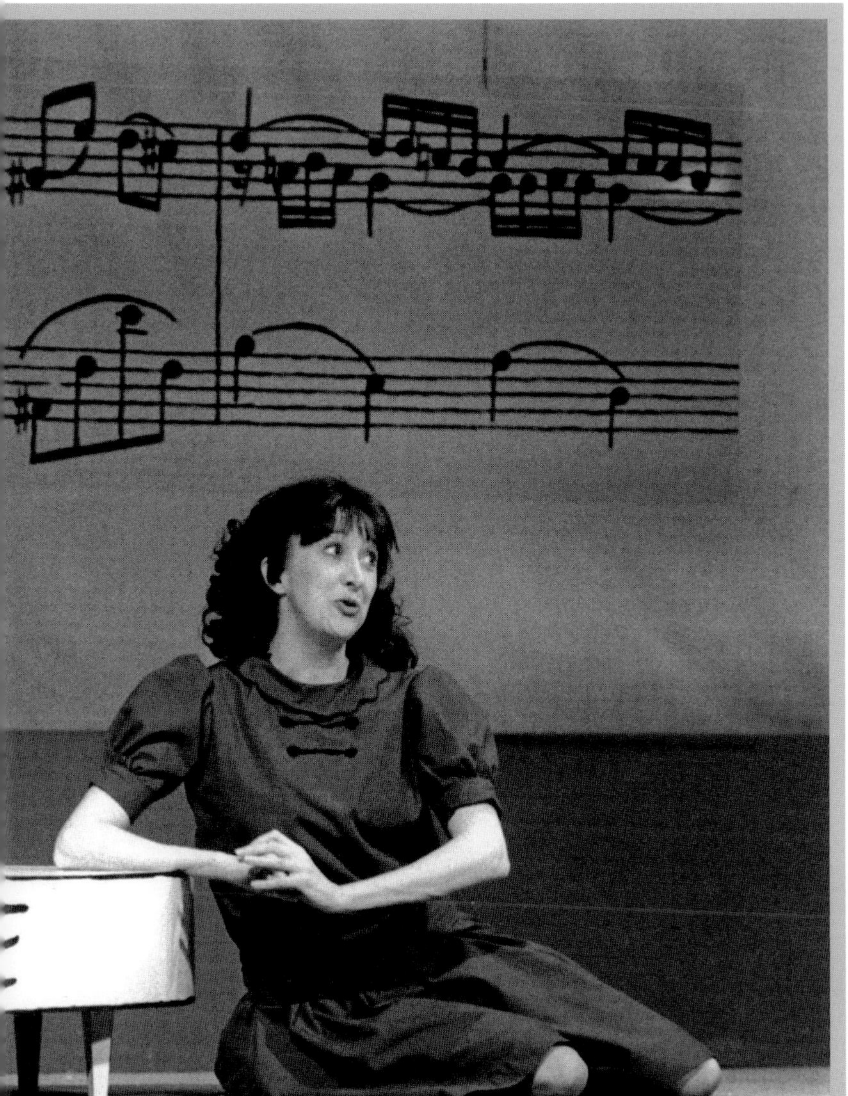

sh, lifted a voice, banged a drum, or simply paused to watch and learn.

- Brooks Smith and Wayne Dementi

1530 Oak Grove Drive
Manakin-Sabot, VA 23103

ISBN: 978-0-9823348-7-4

Brooks Smith & Wayne Dementi
Co-authors

For information write:

Dementi Milestone Publishing
1530 Oak Grove Drive
Manakin-Sabot, VA 23103

dementi@aol.com or (804) 784-5151

Jayne Hushen, Graphic Design

Cover image
On The Waterfront. By Ed Trask. This work was commissioned by Venture Richmond for the 2008 Richmond Folk Festival.

THE

SONGLINES of RICHMOND

A Celebration of Performing Arts, Artists and Stages

Foreword

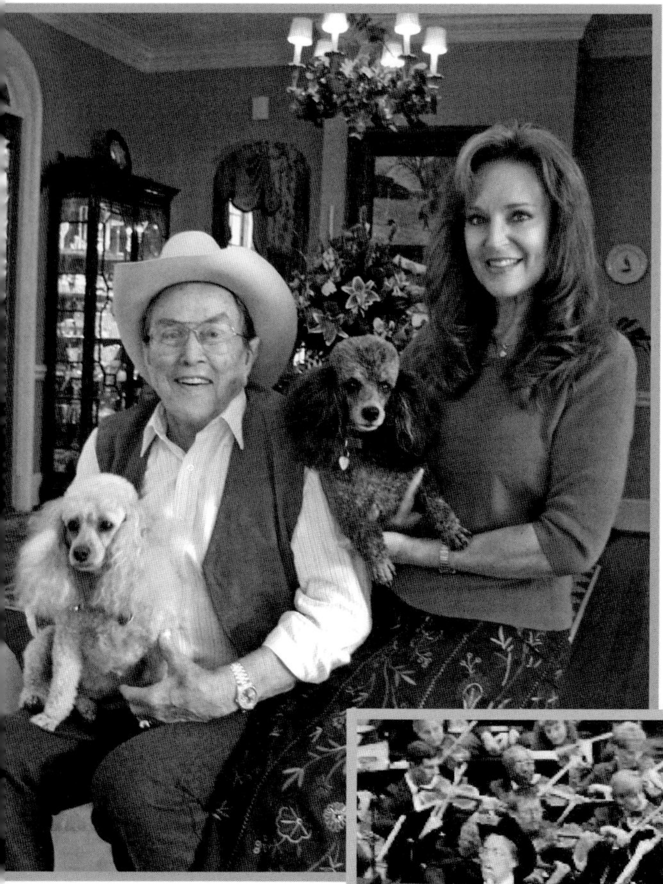

In 1990, Jimmy Dean married fellow performer and songwriter Donna Meade and moved from his home in New Jersey to a tranquil area on the banks of the James River just outside of Richmond. He and Donna have become some of the community's most civic-minded citizens, sponsoring incentive programs in the area's high school and elementary schools. In June of 1997, Jimmy was inducted into Virginia's Country Music Hall of Fame.

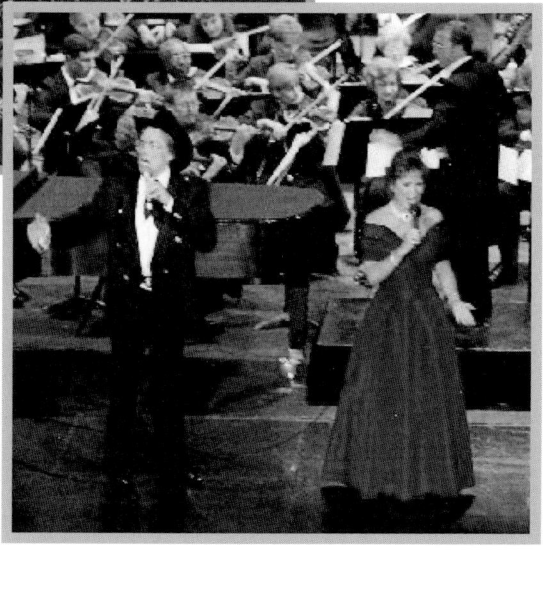

Since 1990, my wife Donna and I have enjoyed living at what we call "the sweetest place on Earth," our home on the James River just outside of Richmond. Being a part of the rural community known as Varina has always been important to us, and in the mid-90's, Donna and I decided to become benefactors of our local Varina High School. We formed the Dean Foundation and sponsored an incentive program for students and teachers called *The Dean's List.* Our program bought much needed items not included in the county's budget such as band uniforms and an activity bus, and gave away savings bonds, school jackets, cash, and even new cars.

As a personal gift to the school, I decided to write their *alma mater*, and I ended up with a melody and the lyrics, "Varina, Dear Old Varina... how proudly we wear your gold and blue." Shortly thereafter, Donna played it for her family at her mother's house, and they liked the song so much that one of her brother's remarked, "That's too good to be a school song... you should make it something bigger." Donna thought for a moment and said "Okay," turned back to the piano and began to sing, "Virginia, Dear Old Virginia... there's no place on Earth I'd rather be...." That night, our song "Virginia" was born, and a few hours later Donna had finished composing the lyrics.

After a lot of positive response to the song, Donna and I recorded a CD of "Virginia." Folks began asking where they could buy a copy, and since we felt kind of badly that Varina High School never got their *alma mater*, we sold the CDs for a few dollars and put the money right back into the Dean Foundation. It was a win-win situation, as Donna and I ended up with our heartfelt tribute to the most beautiful place we know... Virginia, Dear Old Virginia... there's no place on Earth we'd rather be.

Donna and I are so happy to be part of this community, and to celebrate the musical storylines, or "songlines" as Wayne and Brooks call them, that make the Richmond area such a vibrant place for performing arts and artists. Some of them are preserved in this book. We hope that as you read it, you will remember others who deserve to be added to our collective celebration.

Preface

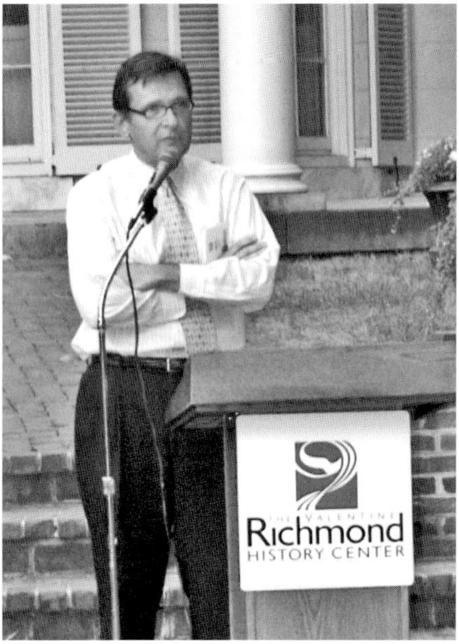

Over the last decade, the Richmond region has witnessed dramatic changes in its cultural life. We've celebrated the creation of new organizations such as CenterStage (with its renovation of the historic Loew's Theatre), the American Civil War Center, and the First Fridays Art Walk, and we've witnessed the transformation of the Richmond Ballet, the Children's Museum of Richmond, Lewis Ginter Botanical Gardens, Maymont, the Visual Arts Center, and the Virginia Historical Society through major capital improvements. The reopening of the expanded Virginia Museum of Fine Arts in 2010 (when it will become one of the nation's largest art museums), continues the remarkable growth of the region's cultural life.

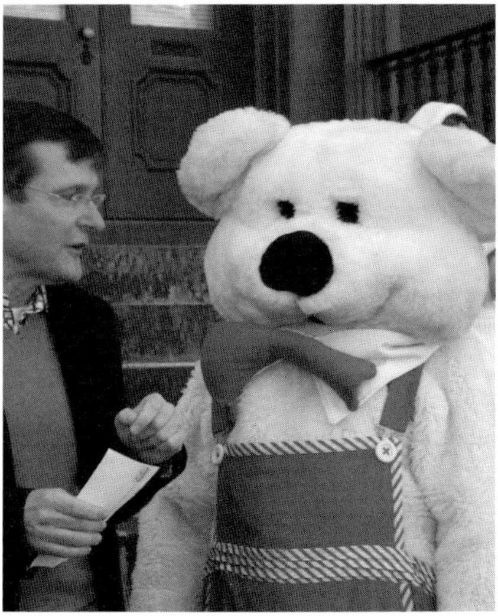

Others, like Theatre IV and the Valentine Richmond History Center, have creatively joined with organizations with similar missions and programs for their further growth and development. Virginia

Commonwealth University's School of the Arts is recognized as one of the premier arts programs in the country.

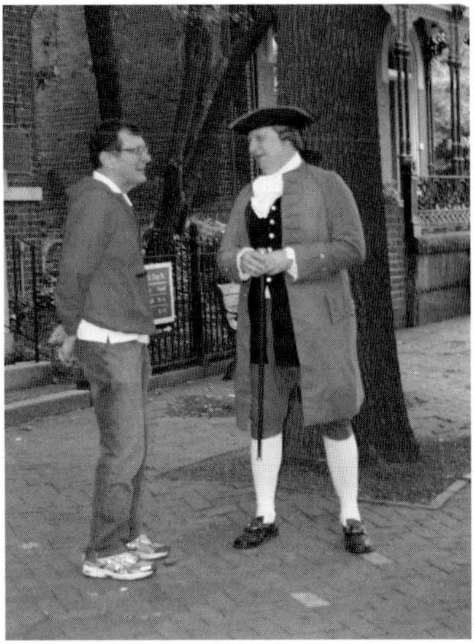

Arts and culture are flourishing beyond the city limits. Chesterfield County has historic Magnolia Grange and the Chesterfield Historical Society. Henrico boasts the vibrant Glen Allen Cultural Arts Center and Meadow Farm. The performing arts and history merge at Hanover Tavern in Hanover County, and the Richmond Symphony, the Virginia Opera, the Richmond Jazz Society, and the Latin Ballet have all found enthusiastic audiences across the greater Richmond area.

The creative process runs beyond the walls of theaters, museums, historic sites, and galleries. Individual artists and emerging art and performance spaces flourish around us, with developments on Broad and Main Streets and in Manchester and Shockoe Bottom. The region's libraries and recreation facilities, churches and street corners brim with cultural programming.

Richmond's creative impulse has always been present; its energy lifts our spirits, affirms our best values, and inspires our everyday lives. *The Songlines of Richmond* not only reminds us of our rich cultural heritage, but also provides a hint of the people and places that are at its source.

Bill Martin

Director, Valentine Richmond History Center

ABOUT THE AUTHORS

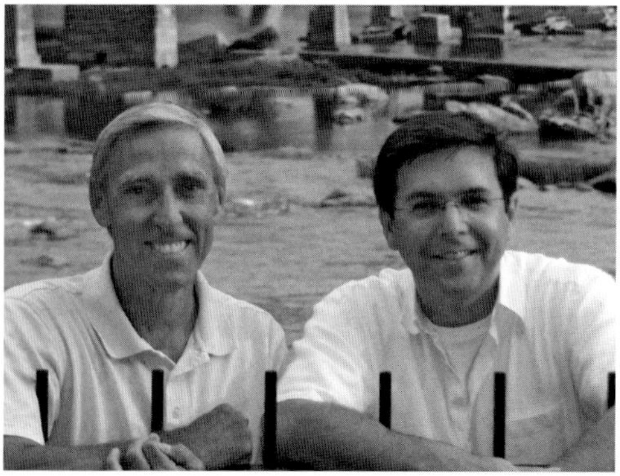

Brooks Smith is a lawyer by profession and a writer by heart. His essays, which have aired regularly on WCVE Public Radio since 2005, celebrate the nearly forgotten storylines of Richmond.

Whether on air or in print, Brooks' writing is whimsical, irregular, and perhaps even prose-like. Wayne Farrar, WCVE Public Radio's News Director, once described Brooks as having "the tenacity of a historian, the curiosity of a journalist, and the soul of a poet."

If any of this is true, then Brooks ascribes it to the soulful City he calls home, where stories seem to accrete on the banks of the James like so many pieces of driftwood. Brooks practices environmental law at Hunton & Williams LLP, and lives in Richmond's Fan District with his wife, Jennifer, and two children, Emma and Ethan.

Wayne Dementi is a photographer, past president of Dementi Studio, and member of a family of photographers that has been capturing Richmond's most iconic landmarks and people for nearly a century. Wayne released his first book, *Celebrate Richmond*, in the fall of 1999. The book quickly became a best seller, and inspired Wayne to author or collaborate on over fifteen other books in the past decade.

Wayne is as accomplished at storytelling as he is at camera work, and his tales of old and forgotten Richmond have delighted audiences far and near. Wayne lives in rural Goochland County with his wife, Dianne. Their grown children adventure around Richmond just like Wayne did as a child, driving ever so slowly with his dad to capture that perfect streak of light, or air, or cover of cloud.

Brooks and Wayne also co-authored *Facts and Legends of the Hills of Richmond*, which was released in the fall of 2008.

About the Artist

You may not know Ed Trask, but you surely know his paintings and murals, which grace halls and walls throughout our fair City and beyond. His brush strokes are unmistakably bold and rhythmic, and his scenes evoke familiar but almost forgotten themes of preservation, spirituality, and social equity. It is impossible to pass by one of Ed's works without being drawn into his kaleidoscope skies, confused telephone wires, grit-stained freight cars, graffiti, or faces made real and alive – almost family – by the touch of Ed's paint-dabbled hand.

For his first gallery, Ed chose the old, dilapidated buildings downtown and around the VCU campus, reviving them, and us, with his larger than life murals. Ed's paintings now hang in permanent collections all around the world, including Gap, Capitol One, Old Navy, Fortune Magazine, NBC, Ducati, St. Laurent, Philip Morris, Media General, and Play Inc.

Ed is a graduate of VCU's School of the Arts. He lives in Richmond with his wife and two children. In addition to art, Ed is a gifted musician. He has banged his drum with the Holly Rollers and Kepone, and more recently, Avail and Corntooth.

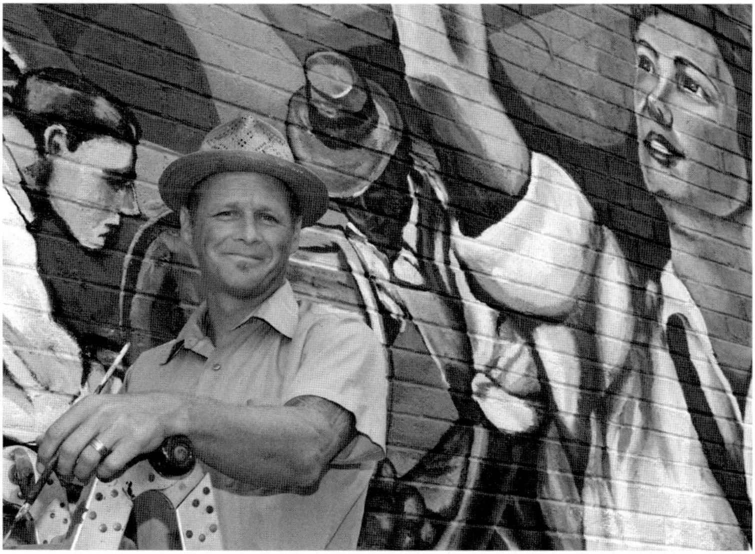

Affirmations

Since 1986, I've had the privilege of welcoming over 800,000 children to the historic Empire Theatre for a Theatre IV production. During the recent run of "Annie," a young mother came up to me with her own two children, and told me that Theatre IV provided many of her happiest childhood memories. She turned to her children and said, "When I was your age, I was always afraid to come downtown. This is the man who made me feel at home down here." I couldn't have been more flattered.

Phil Whiteway, Managing Director,
Theatre IV - The Children's Theatre of Virginia

The arts enable us to see our world and ourselves through an amazing range of lenses. Priority attention to arts attendance and participation provides unmatched benefits to our personal and professional lives.

John Bryan, President, CultureWorks
(formerly known as the Arts Council of Richmond)

When talking to longtime Symphony-goers and supporters, you find that there is always a specific instance or story that led to their sustained interest in the organization and the music. "I remember the first time I heard the Richmond Symphony" or "My wife and I have been attending concerts for over thirty years." The Symphony is more than musical entertainment to most patrons – it's an integral part of their identity and experience of living in the City of Richmond. We (the Richmond Symphony) take pride in shaping the quality of life in the community.

David J.L. Fisk, Executive Director, Richmond Symphony

Jazz music is like a "balm in Gilead" – it heals the soul and soothes the wounded heart. And, in the last thirty years, through the efforts of Richmond Jazz Society, it has provided a unique source of synergy for our City. I believe that this music has touched so many people in such a deeply emotional way, that it has woven a richer tapestry of racial, social, and economic diversity among our citizens than any other art form. Since its formation in 1979, the Richmond Jazz Society has grown to be the premier jazz service organization for Richmond and the Commonwealth of Virginia through our mission to educate, preserve, and advance this music as an American art form. We are still learning about Richmond's integral role in the historical development of jazz, and our local connections to some of the music's greatest innovators and performers. Jazz is a source of inspiration and creativity for our youth, and a wellspring of joy and bright moments for our seniors. Jazz is America's music. Richmond continues to play a vital role in its current emanations; in the preservation of its historical significance; and in the investment for its future.

B. J. Brown, Executive Director, Richmond Jazz Society

I love performing with the Latin Ballet because, in addition to bringing a unique type of dance to Richmond that balances the "dance especially for entertainment" element with "dance as an art form" element, there is an enthusiasm and a love among the dancers that is catching. The Latin Ballet introduces performing to dancers of all ages. I've seen the youngest children learn responsibility, love of craft, "doing one's best" as well as creativity and pride in same.

Frances Wessells, Associate Professor Emerita, VCU Dance, and Visiting Artist, Latin Ballet

Seeing a good dancer makes us feel good about being alive. It demonstrates human beings at their very best. The dancer takes only her God-given equipment – body and soul – and hones both to the highest possible height. A dancer accepts the physical trials of an athlete and the emotional challenges of an artist, then combines these in her instrument, herself, to become the most powerful poster child possible for the glory of humankind, thus uplifting the hearts of those who watch. At Richmond Ballet, our mission – "to awaken and uplift the human spirit through dance" – is at the heart of every performance we present and every class we teach.

Stoner Winslett, Artistic Director, Richmond Ballet

It was my dream as a kid to spend my life making music for people. The Virginia music scene has allowed me to do that since 1962. Thank you Virginia! I pray the coming years will allow today's young artists and musicians the opportunities and support I have enjoyed.

Steve Bassett, Virginia music artist

Not many people are fortunate enough to make a living doing something that they absolutely love to do. I happen to be one of those fortunate people. Writing and performing music has been my job for over 40 years. I doubt if I could say this without the support of Virginians and the inspiration of living here in The Sweet Virginia Breeze.

Robbin Thompson, Virginia singer / songwriter

We Virginians try for restraint when it comes to singing the praises of our Commonwealth. But let's face it, distinguished sons and daughters in the music world include Shirley MacLaine, Jimmy Dean, and Bill Robinson (Mr. Bojangles). Our proud and charming capital city, Richmond, has hosted, nurtured, and preserved an astonishing variety of music, music halls, theaters, concert halls, and festivals celebrating everything from tidewater blues to mountain gospel, opera, and honky-tonk. Modesty? We wouldn't know the meaning of the word!

Earl Hamner, Virginia actor, writer and producer

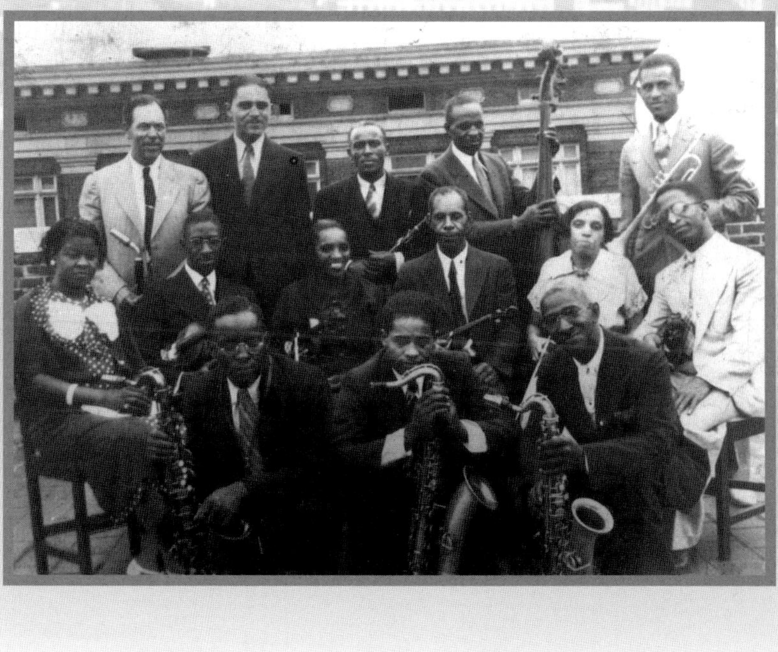

INTRODUCTION

For all you grammarians out there, "songlines" is not a real word, at least not one that you'll find defined in the dictionary. "Songlines" is a feeling, a meditation. It is a dream that originates with the distant Aborigines of Australia, who believed that we must make a song out of everything we see, and in so doing, make what we see real. These songs guide the paths of our daily lives. They direct us, caution us, and sometimes turn us around. It may be true that we need food more than song, but when you are struggling with loss, or trying to find your footing, or simply lost along the way, the lilting chords of a human voice will sustain you far beyond the most plentiful feast.

The songlines of Richmond run deep. They extend back to the earliest days of our native peoples, and sideways to every genre of sound inspired by what we have seen or experienced. Our songlines also run forward. They are at the core of our cultural fabric. And beyond money, or rank, or condition, they alone have the power to transform our fair little City.

This book is not an encyclopedia. It surely omits songs that deserve to be sung. But in the black ink of words and images that follow, we hope to share a few stories about performing arts, artists, and stages in Richmond that help to line the paths of our past, and perhaps also, our future.

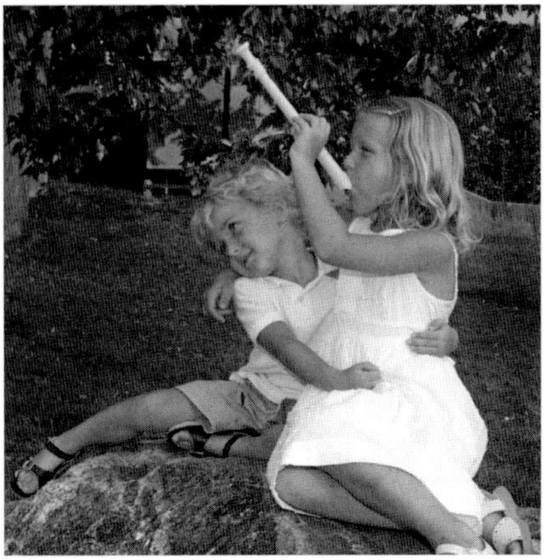

The people we met along the way inspired us. Their stories made us weep, laugh, hope, and dream about this place we call home. They opened our eyes to the old crooners who sit on lonely street corners, to the young kids who beat out their symphonies on upturned pails, and even to the passing strangers who through some murmur of song or rat-a-tat tapping of feet become as dear as family.

In the course of exploring old songlines and uncovering new ones, we learned a few meditations worth sharing. Laugh when you can. Smile when you pass, even if it is just a dog. If you can walk, you can dance. If you can talk, you can sing. And if you are too tired to do anything more than watch or listen, then watch or listen.

Richmond is a special place. It is filled with important, austere things. But it is also filled with song. And that is what this little book seeks to celebrate.

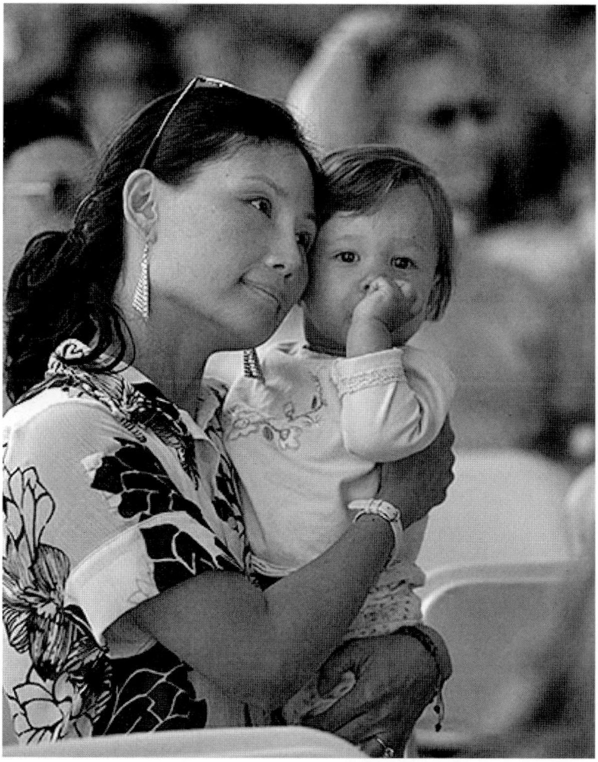

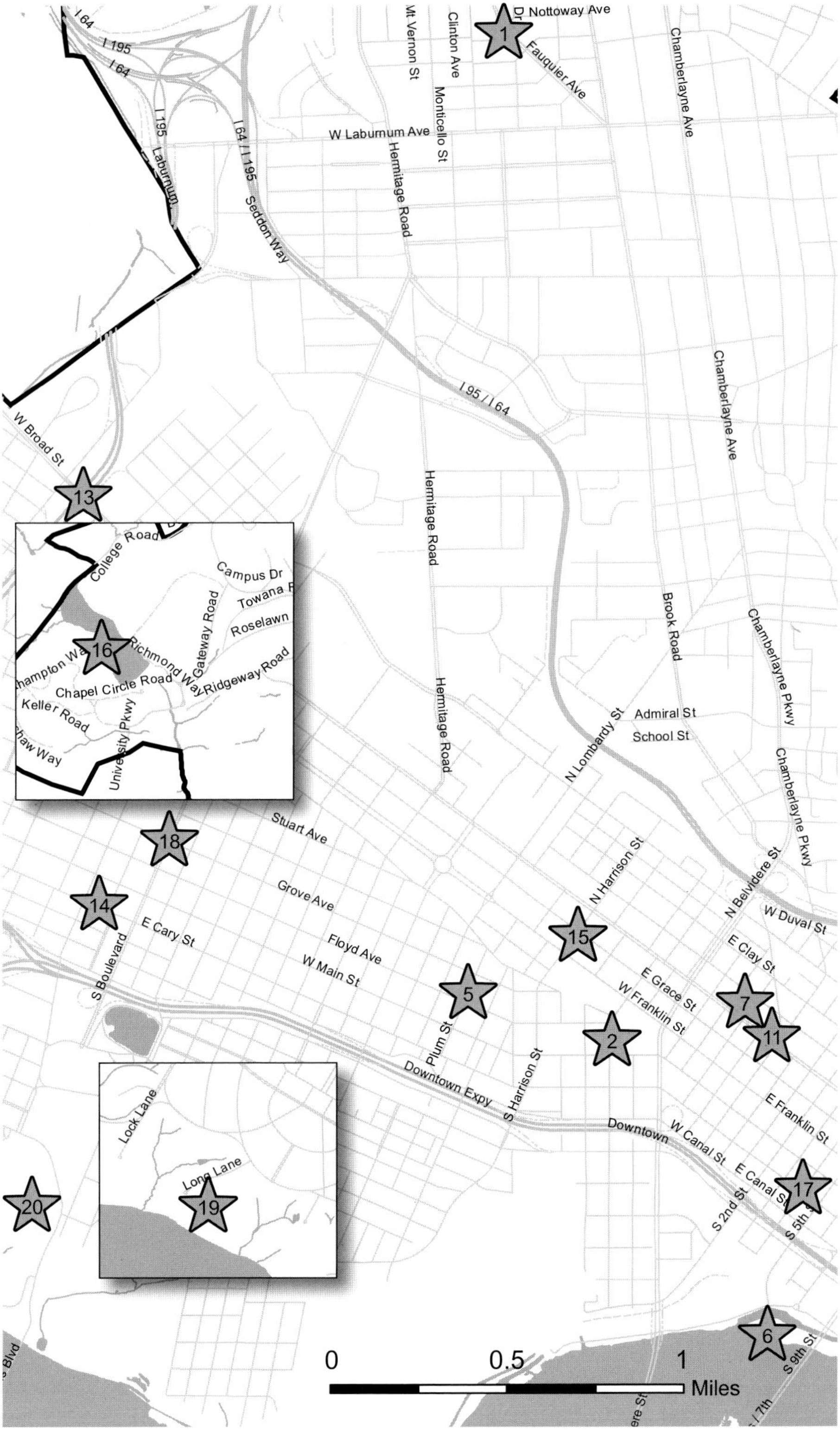

Nottoway Ave
Dr
1
Fauquier Ave
Mt Vernon St
Clinton Ave
Chamberlayne Ave
I 64
I 195
I 64
Monticello St
I 195
W Laburnum Ave
I 64 / I 195
Laburnum
Hermitage Road
Seddon Way
I 95 / I 64
Chamberlayne Ave
W Broad St
13
Hermitage Road
College Road
Campus Dr
Towana R
Gateway Road
Roselawn
16
Richmond Way
Ridgeway Road
Chapel Circle Road
Keller Road
University Pkwy
Brook Road
Chamberlayne Pkwy
Hermitage Road
Admiral St
School St
N Lombardy St
Chamberlayne Pkwy
Stuart Ave
18
N Harrison St
N Belvidere St
Grove Ave
14
W Duval St
15
E Cary St
Floyd Ave
E Clay St
W Main St
E Grace St
7
S Boulevard
5
W Franklin St
11
2
Plum St
Downtown Expy
S Harrison St
E Franklin St
Lock Lane
Downtown
W Canal St
Long Lane
E Canal St
17
20
19
S 2nd St
S 5th
6
S 9th St
0
0.5
1
Miles

ADVENTURE MAP

1. Shirley MacLaine's Childhood Home
2. Mosque/Landmark Theatre
3. Lyric/WRVA Theatre
4. The Deuce
5. Artist Colony on Plum Street
6. Folk Festival Environs
7. 1708 Gallery/Broad Street Arts and Cultural District
8. Quesnay's Academy
9. Robinson Theater
10. Loew's Movie Palace/Carpenter Center/Richmond CenterStage
11. Theatre IV/Maggie Walker/Booker T
12. The National
13. Tantilla Garden
14. The Byrd Theatre
15. Virginia Commonwealth University
16. University of Richmond
17. Richmond Ballet
18. Virginia Museum of Fine Arts
19. Richmond Shakespeare at Agecroft Hall
20. Dogwood Dell
21. Richmond Coliseum

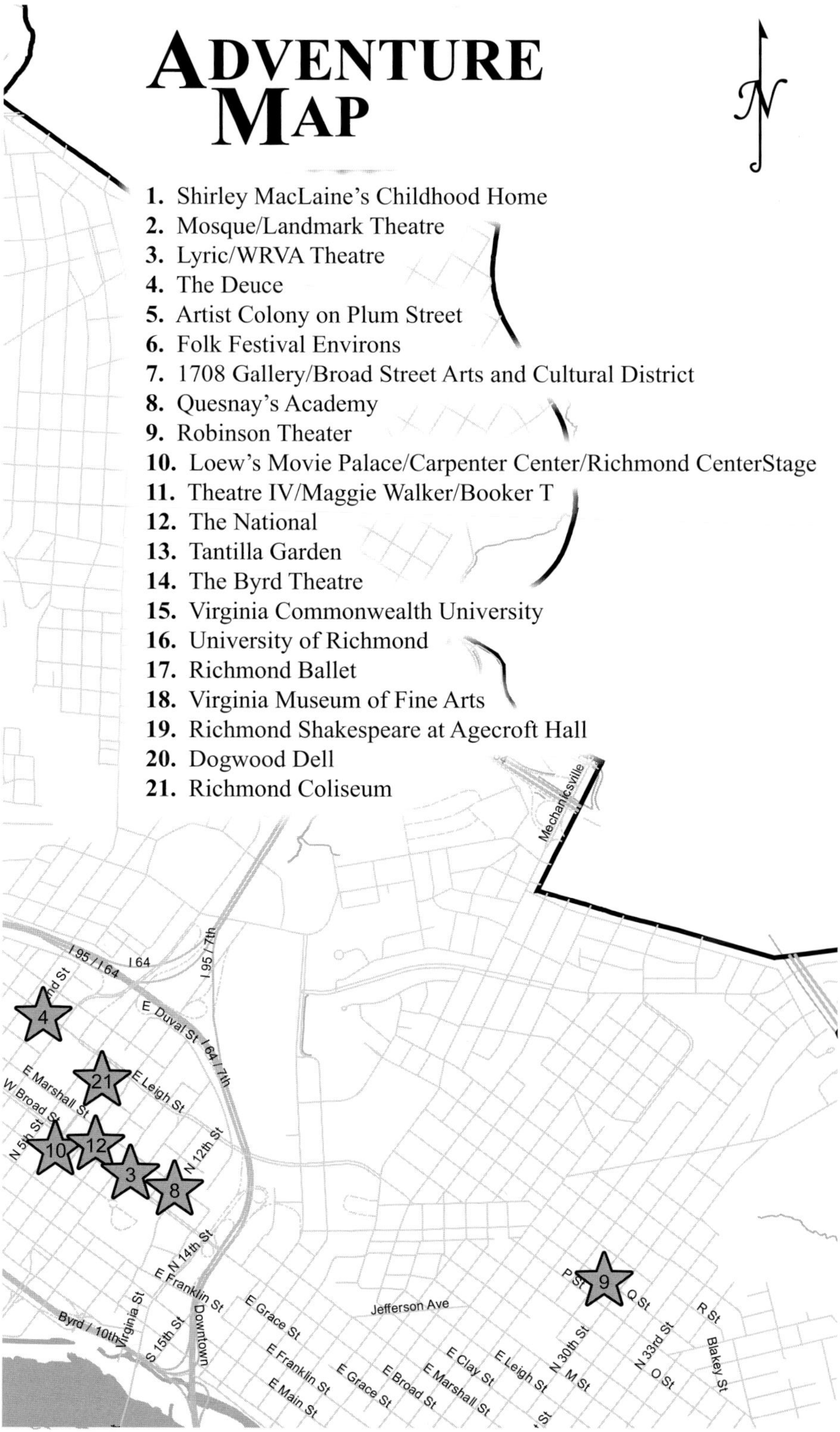

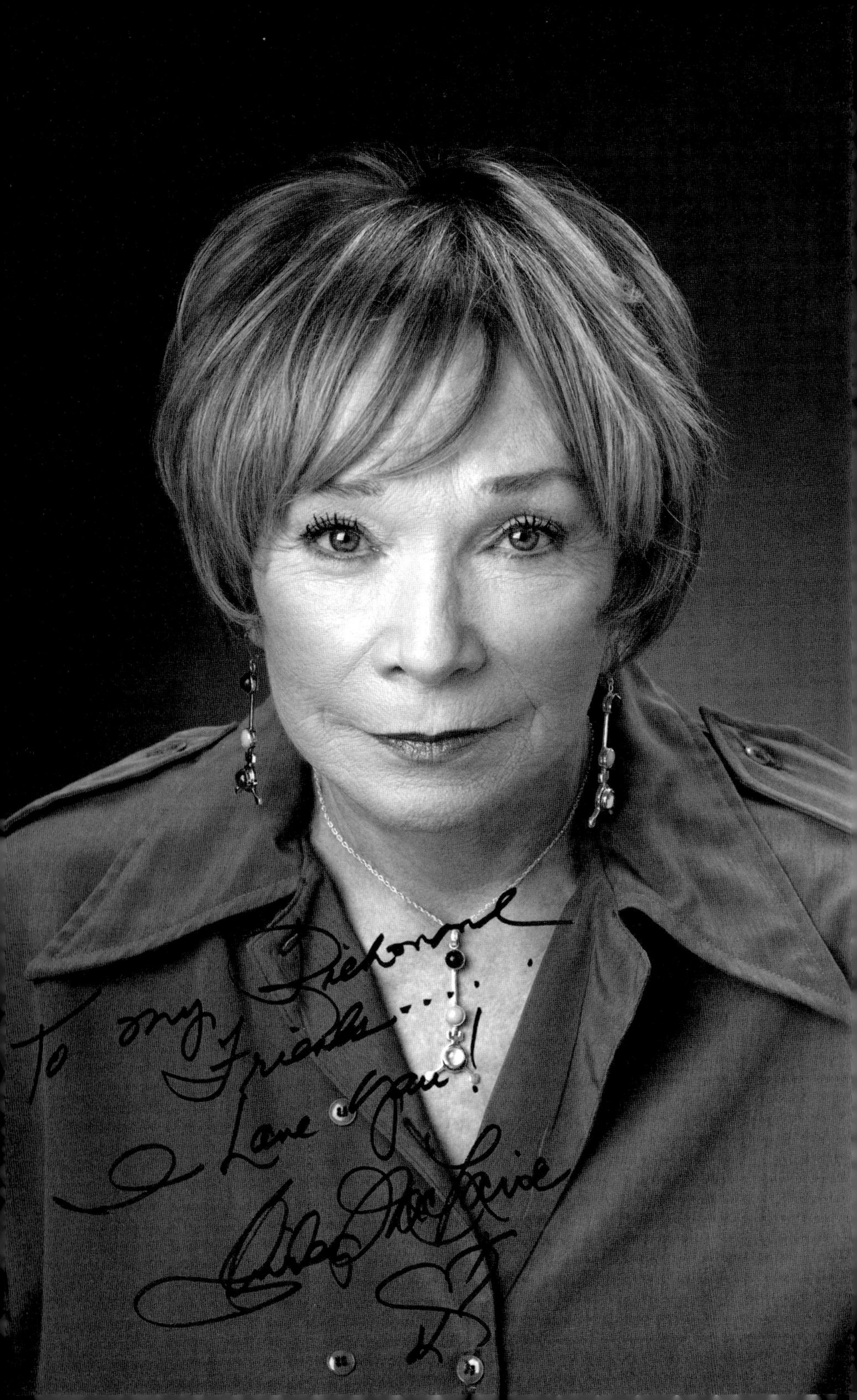
To my Richmond Friends....
I Love You!
Shirley MacLaine

SHIRLEY MACLAINE

We all search for angels, and I think Shirley MacLaine must have found them. Or so it would seem as you study the prismatic arc of her career as an Academy Award-winning actress, best-selling author, roving world traveler, and new-age spiritualist. But ask her about this and she will refer all of her successes back to her formative years in Richmond, Virginia.

Ms. MacLaine was born Shirley MacLean Beaty on April 24, 1934. Her father was a principal at Westhampton School, and her mother was a drama coach and actress. They lived on Park Avenue in the Westhampton neighborhood, and then on Fauquier Avenue in Bellevue.

Some of Shirley's fondest childhood memories involve movies at the Bellevue Theatre, where she and her now equally famous brother, Warren, liked to go after school. "We would have gone every day if we could," Shirley reflects. "And I loved every movie I ever saw."

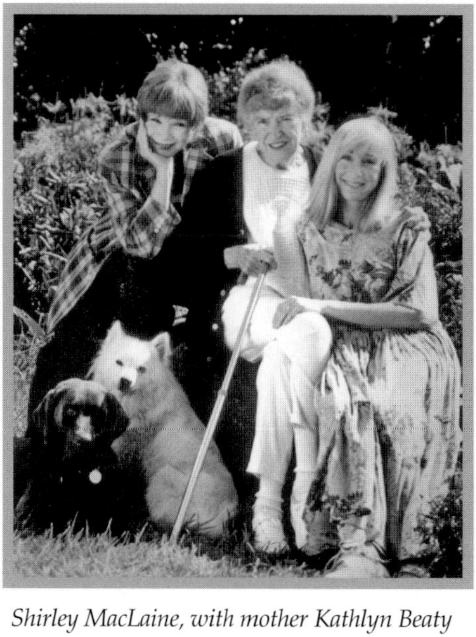

Shirley MacLaine, with mother Kathlyn Beaty and daughter, Sachi Parker. 1991.

But Shirley's mother had other plans for her, including the systematic strengthening of her wobbly ankles. At the age of two, Shirley was

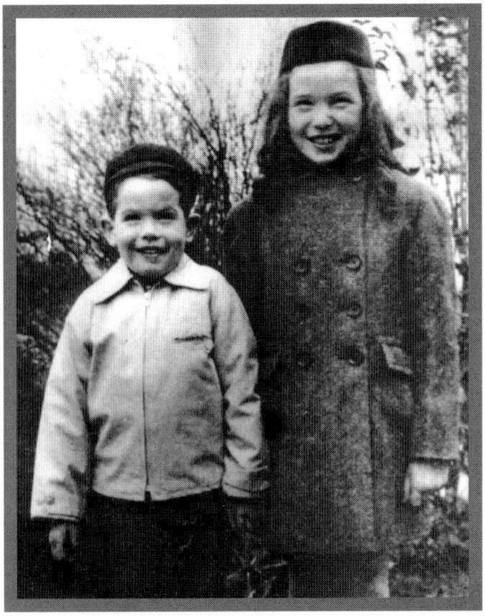

Childhood photo of Shirley MacLaine with her brother, Warren Beatty.

enrolled into Julia Mildred Harper's School of Dance in Ginter Park. By all accounts a disciplinarian, Ms. Harper was also a gifted teacher. As Shirley recalls, "she taught us to use our hands so that we might be graceful from the arms down. And that, of course, is the key to success." In dance, like many other things, success came very early for Shirley. At the ripe old age of four, she made her first stage appearance before a live audience at the Mosque.

Of course, all of this is obscured by the famous firsts that followed: Broadway debut at age 16; movie debut in Hitchcock's *The Trouble with Harry* at age 21; co-starring role with the Rat Packers in *Ocean's Eleven* at age 26; and first book at age 35. Shirley's credits have gone on to include over 50 movies, 10 books, and an Academy Award for her performance in *Terms of Endearment.*

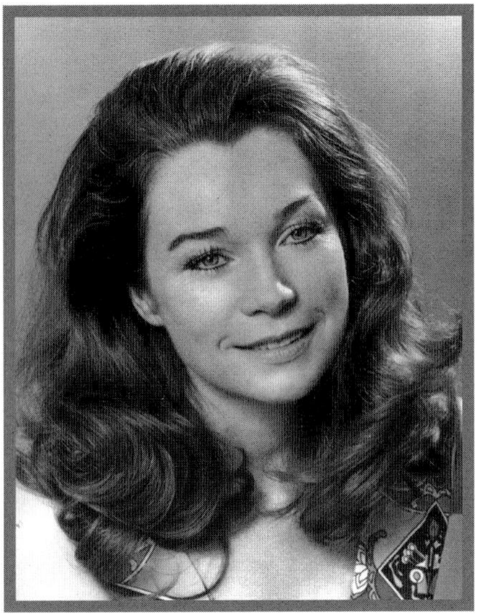

The movie I remember best is the one my father embraced with near religious fervor during my childhood, the impossibly funny *Being There*. In the movie, Shirley co-starred with Peter Sellers in the late-great comedian's finest and final role as Chance the gardener. On screen and off, Sellers exuded a "peculiar form of optimism" that must have been infectious, because Shirley carries it forward.

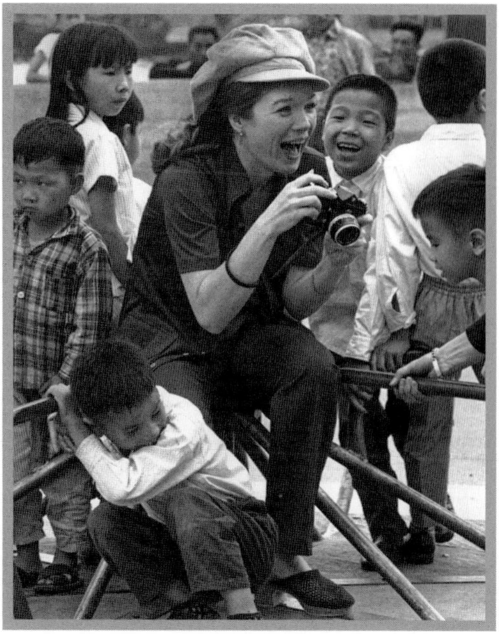

Shirley MacLaine on a photojournalism trip to Hong Kong.

She remembers with near bliss a tree by her childhood home, a tree she named Rover, a name that is now a metaphor for her roving life. The tree was a confidant to a young Shirley still struggling to find her way in the world. She will never forget that tree, or her formative years here. As she begged me to report, "Tell everybody from my home, I love them."

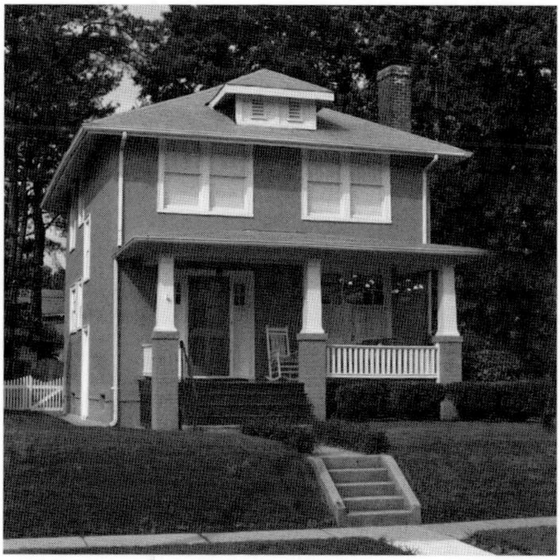

Childhood home of Shirley MacLaine in Richmond's Bellevue neighborhood.

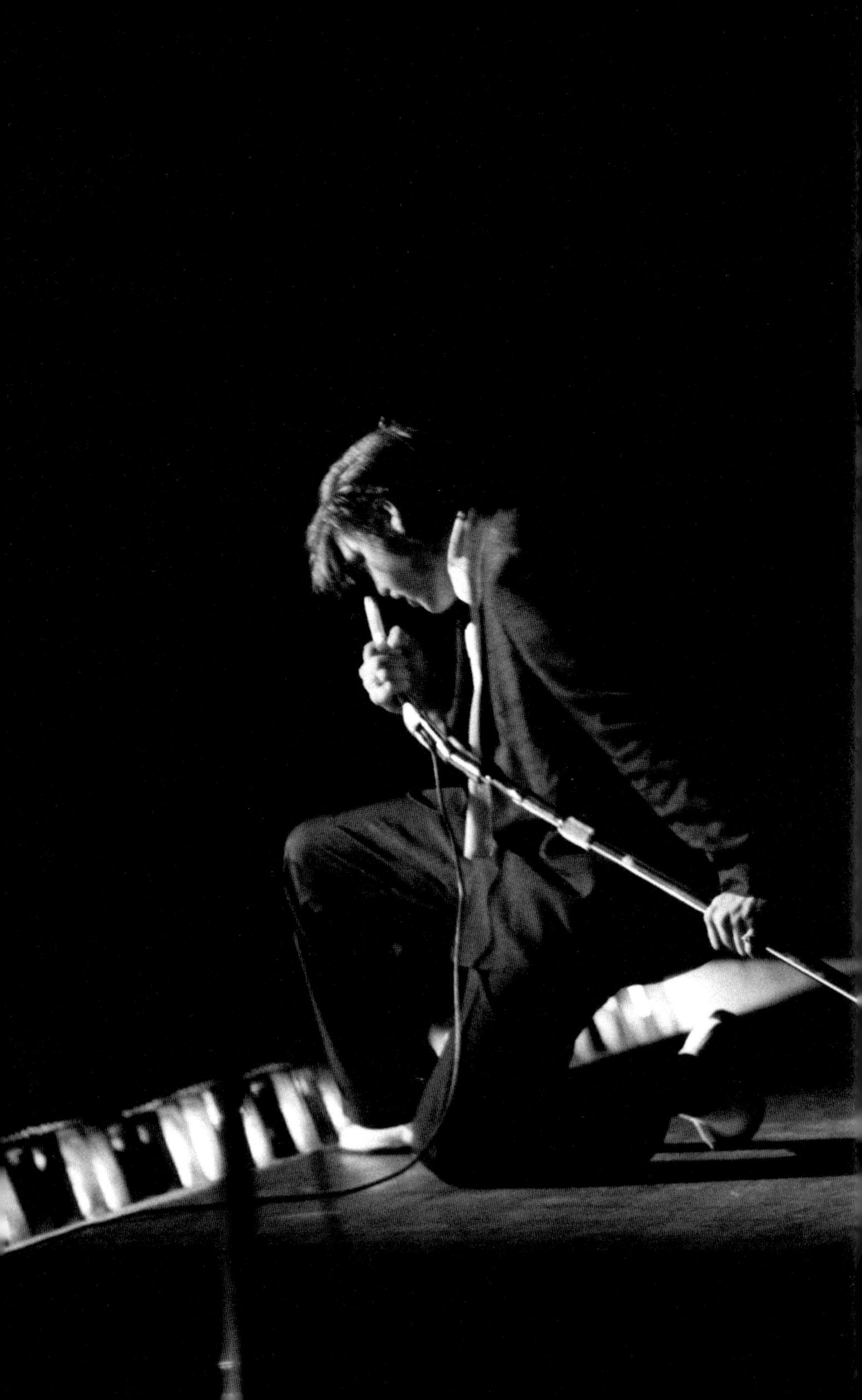

THE KING WAS HERE

On May 16, 1955, Railey's Appliance Center sponsored Hank Snow and his All-Star Hillbilly Jamboree at the Mosque. Snow was a fan favorite from his many local appearances and juke-box recordings. His cast included well-known performers from the Grand Ole Opry like Martha Carson and Slim Whitman. Snow's cast also included a fresh voice out of Memphis, a newcomer named Elvis Presley. The show was a dollar fifty for reserved seating, and a dollar for general admission.

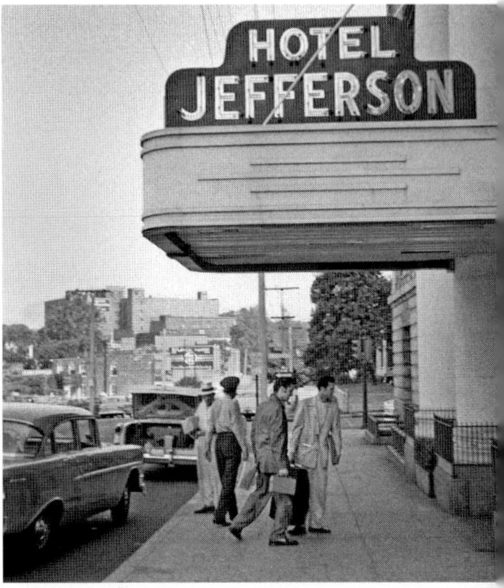

Elvis enters Hotel Jefferson after taking a cab from the Richmond train station. June 30, 1956.

According to the *Times-Dispatch*, Elvis received the "greatest ovation ever" during this first appearance, and he was quickly booked for more. He returned to Richmond in September and November 1955, performing first at the WRVA Theatre and then at a special event for Philip Morris employees.

As the buzz around Elvis continued to intensify, the "King" visited Richmond three more times in 1956. For his February show, the advertisement read: "In person, the sensational new RCA Victor singing star, Elvis Presley, with the Blue Moon Boys and extra Grand Ole Opry favorites." By June, the ad read simply: "Elvis Presley and his stage show." But even then, Elvis had competition. You could

◄ *Elvis Presley in the first of two performances at the Mosque. Elvis is shown kneeling at the footlights before 4,000 mostly teenage female fans. June 30, 1956.*

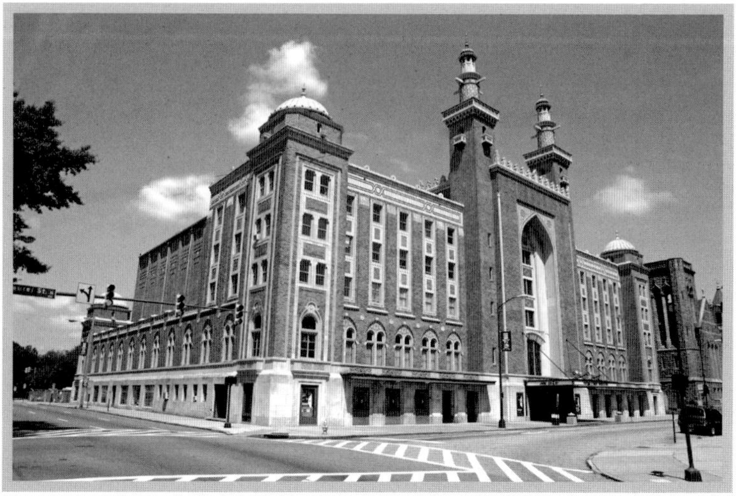

The Landmark Theatre, formerly known as the Mosque, scene of the earliest Elvis performances in Richmond.

have seen Harvey Hudson on the stage of the Byrd Theatre, or *The Last Frontier* at the Bellwood Drive-In for a buck twenty-five a car-full. What kind of car, you ask? Around this time, you could have purchased a spanking new De Soto Firedome for two thousand dollars, or a reliably used '49 Ford for ten times less.

Sadly, after Elvis hit stardom, his visits to Richmond tailed off. But he did give us a few encore performances, the last of which came in June 1976, nearly twenty years to the day after his first headlining show here, and just a year before his untimely end. This Elvis, of course, was different, bound and trussed and addled by his own mortality. But our Richmond audience was ever charitable. We showed up in force – some 11,900 of us – bearing gifts of flowers and hats and hand-lettered signs. According to the *News Leader*, Elvis reciprocated with five kisses and forty-seven scarves. And in the midst of it all, you had this "creepy feeling" that we weren't seeing Elvis as he was then, but rather as he was before, the "sleek, sassy and sexy" King of rock-and-roll with gyrating hips and a voodoo swagger.

Ironically, a year after Elvis died, the Virginia Department of Alcoholic Beverage Control received hundreds of orders for the most expensive novelty item ever sold in a liquor store – a two hundred and twelve dollar "Elvis Gold," a limited edition bourbon decanter dipped in 23-karat gold with a music box that played "My Way," a tragic hit about a man nearing the end of his hard-worn life.

And so the beat goes on. Elvis may have left the building, but his legend abides. And for a few lucky Richmonders among us, Elvis is still that wide-eyed force of nature who debuted here as a hillbilly rocker some fifty-four years ago. If you're out there, this one's for you.

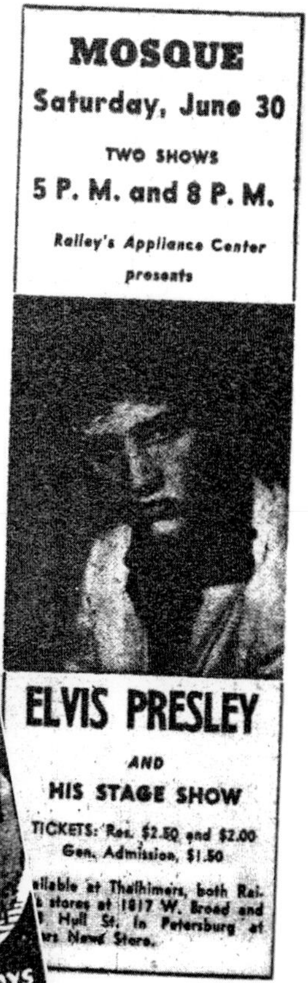

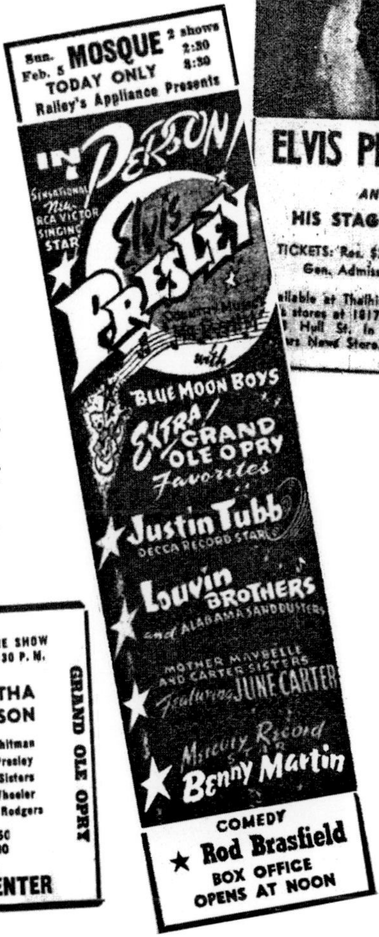

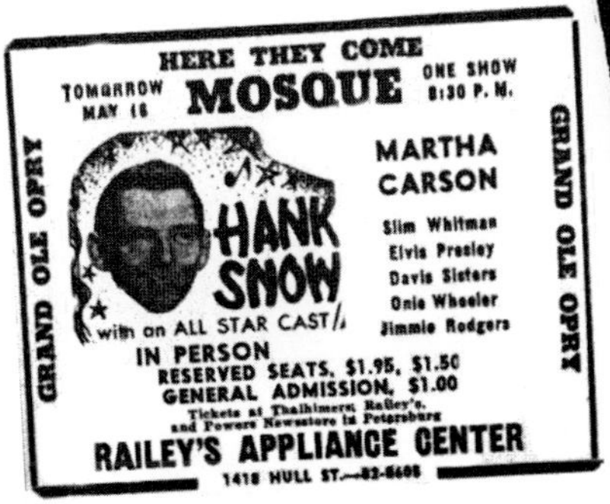

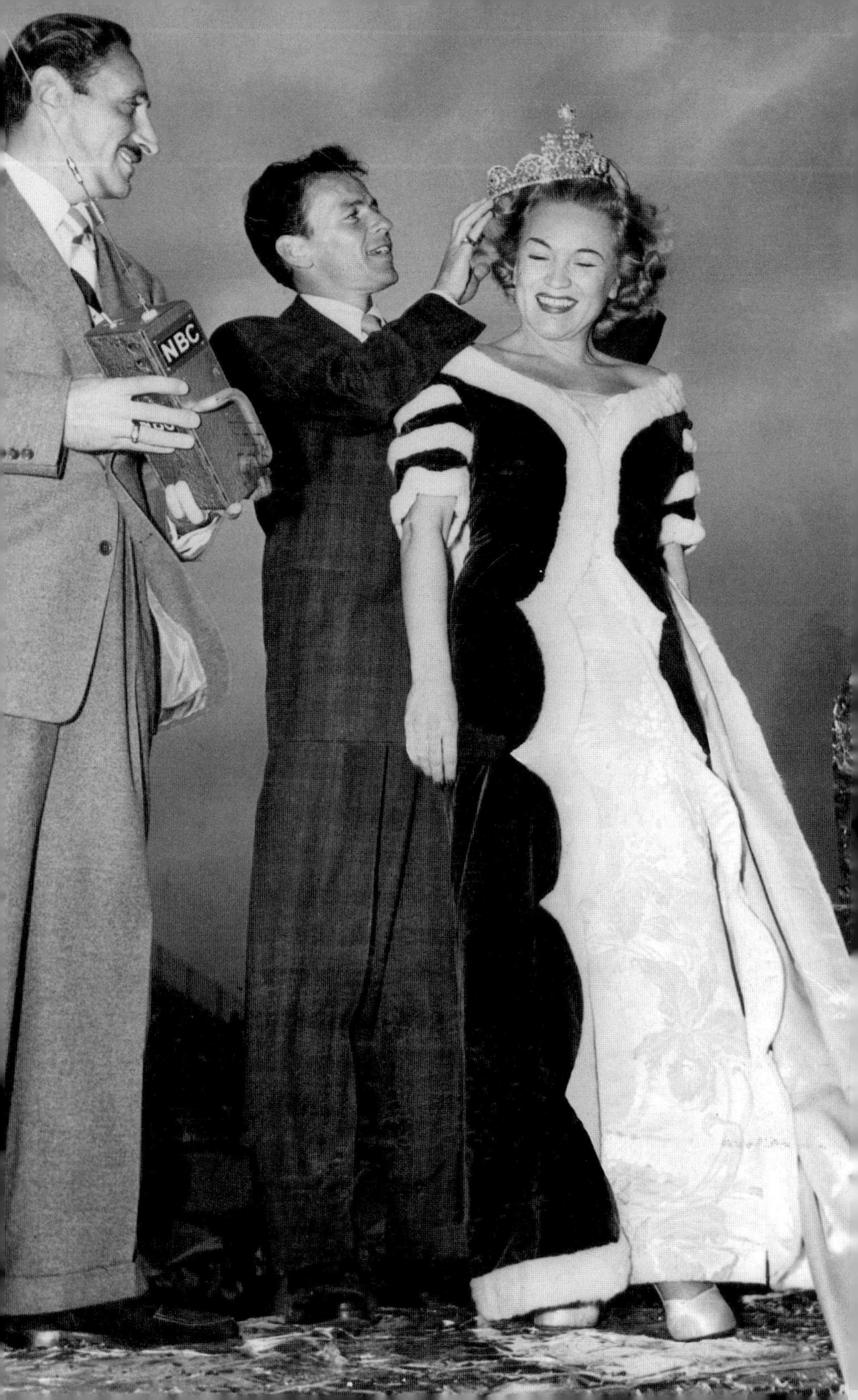
NBC

OL' BLUE EYES

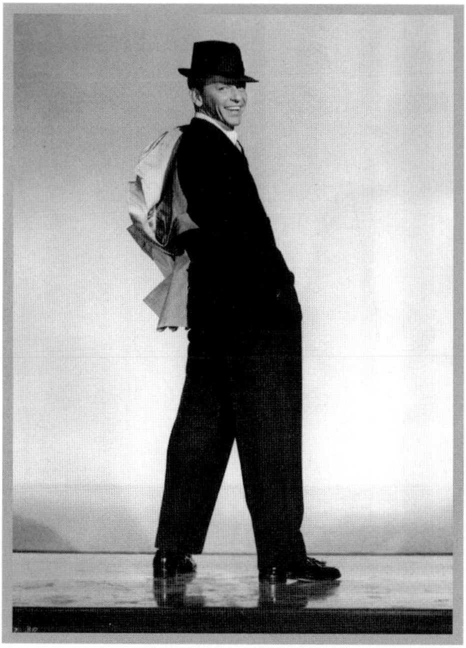

There are many sustained musical forces in Richmond, but every now and again, an incidental guest deserves mention. Take Ol' Blue Eyes – Francis Albert Sinatra – who first appeared here as a gangling, 26-year old songster with the Tommy Dorsey Orchestra on April 27, 1941. Amidst the darkening anxieties of war and a new German offensive into the Mediterranean, Sinatra's visit provided a few hours of relief for rattled Richmonders. As the *News Leader* reported the following Monday, the concert offered an "antidote for the worries that infest this topsy-turvy world."

Sinatra returned four years later to perform as part of a Victory Bond Show. The Voice, as he was then known, brought down the house, delighting his squealing fans with the swoon version of hits like "Night and Day" and "I'll Buy That Dream." WRVA even installed speakers outside of the Mosque so that fans could enjoy the show from Monroe Park, as well as inside the theatre. No doubt the cries of "Ooooooh Frankeeee!" could be heard as far away as the Boulevard. This second visit netted more in "E" bond sales than any previous bond show in Richmond, and was reported

Frank Sinatra crowns Dorothy Kirsten as the first Tobacco Festival Queen on October 15, 1949 in Richmond.

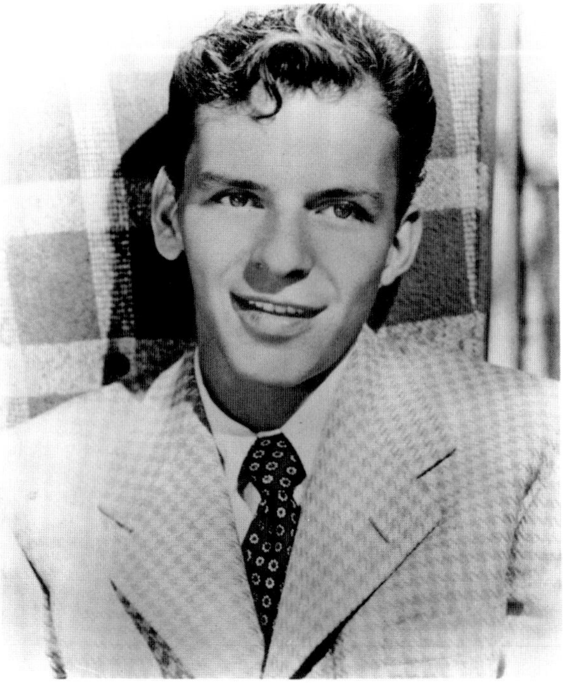

to be "one of the most enjoyable shows ever given here." At the time, Pepsodent tooth powder sold for 39¢ and a Victory Ranger wood tommy gun with the real "ack-ack" sound ran for $1.25.

Sinatra returned for a third visit in 1949, this time as grand marshal of Richmond's first annual Tobacco Bowl Festival. Inspired by the festival's mission to help underprivileged children, Sinatra donated a set of gold cups to the City to be used annually to recognize the Boy and Girl of the Year. He also hosted a breakfast for orphans at the Hotel John Marshall. The festival drew a crowd of 74,000 people and featured parades, performances, and debutante balls, including one at Tantilla Garden with Blue Barron's Orchestra. The festival even featured a nationally televised broadcast of *Hit Parade*, the first time in history that this wildly popular program was recorded outside of Hollywood or New York City. Just beyond the organized festivities, Jackie Robinson's major league All-Stars took on the Richmond Giants at Mooers Field, and up in New York State, 11 "Reds" were convicted of conspiring to overthrow the United States government.

Sinatra's final visit came in 1994. On his first night, the still-crooning 78-year old received seven standing ovations. On his second, he collapsed on stage, was rushed to the hospital, and then withdrew from Richmond for good.

Guests come and go. Few leave lasting marks. Even fewer get a chance to show their own. Sinatra was an exception. He was both the king of the bobby-soxers and a pioneer against prejudice. He mixed his bands before America mixed her people. He gave us zip, zap, zing, and ring-a-ding-ding. In our fair little City, he grew up before our eyes. The "hep cats" may be gone, but the need for respite from a topsy-turvy world remains. As Sinatra liked to toast to his fans, may we all live to be 400 years old, and may the last voice you hear be his.

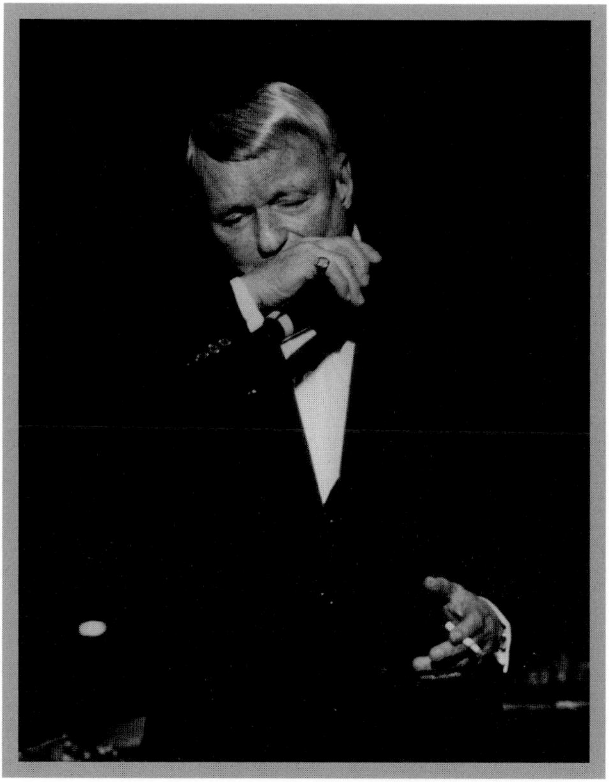

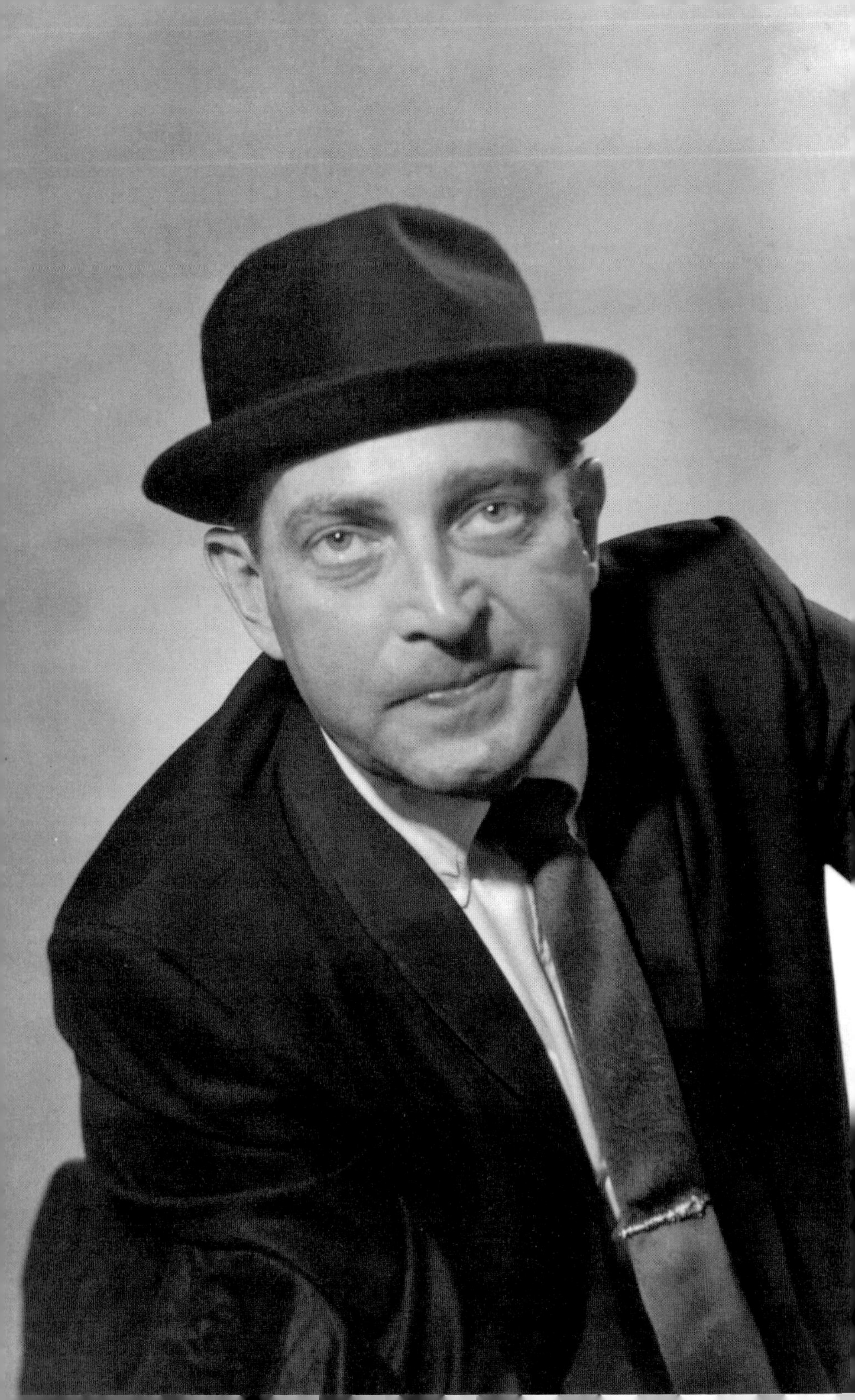

HARVEY HUDSON

Before reality television, there was an improbably endearing medium known as reality radio. Back then, stars were stars, stunts were real, and the stories that were told seemed grander and more spellbinding than any story that could be seen. And the voices, oh the voices! They were like the best of old friends, unmistakably familiar, nearly confidential.

In that league of voices, one has outlasted them all. It belongs to Harvey Hudson, the patriarch of Richmond radio. Harvey began broadcasting in 1940, back when Richmond was a one station city.

One of Harvey's first programs was the *Streitmann's Street Man Show*, broadcast live from just outside of the Loew's Theatre at 6th and Grace. For 15 minutes each morning, Harvey's hostess would mingle in the gathered crowd searching for a few personalities to invite onto the air with Harvey. "Here is so-and-so," she'd offer. "Well hello so-and-so," Harvey would answer. Then, whatever happened, happened. At the end of each *Street Man* interview, Harvey would present his guest with a certificate good for a box of Zesta Crackers, compliments of the Streitmann Biscuit Company.

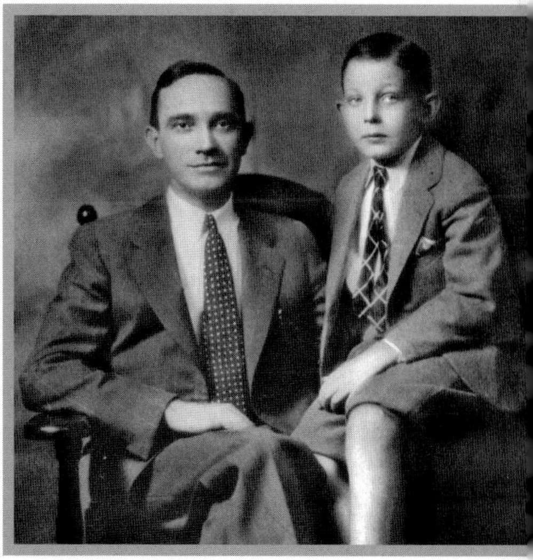

But Harvey was more than just a local morning announcer. He was our beloved clown. When Rockingham introduced the first "light fall" suit, Harvey took it out for a little light fall of his own … from an airplane. And when Freidman Marks started selling "wash and wear" suits, Harvey demonstrated their exceptional qualities by taking a wash and wear dip in the Byrd Park Lake. For a local car dealer, he rode a donkey down Broad Street. His hostess accompanied him with a sign that read: "Harvey Hudson pays off! Commonwealth Ford makes a jackass out of a jackass!" And when a talkie called *Ruthless* hit local screens, Harvey made the title part of every sentence. "My," he'd say. "How ruthless the weather is today!"

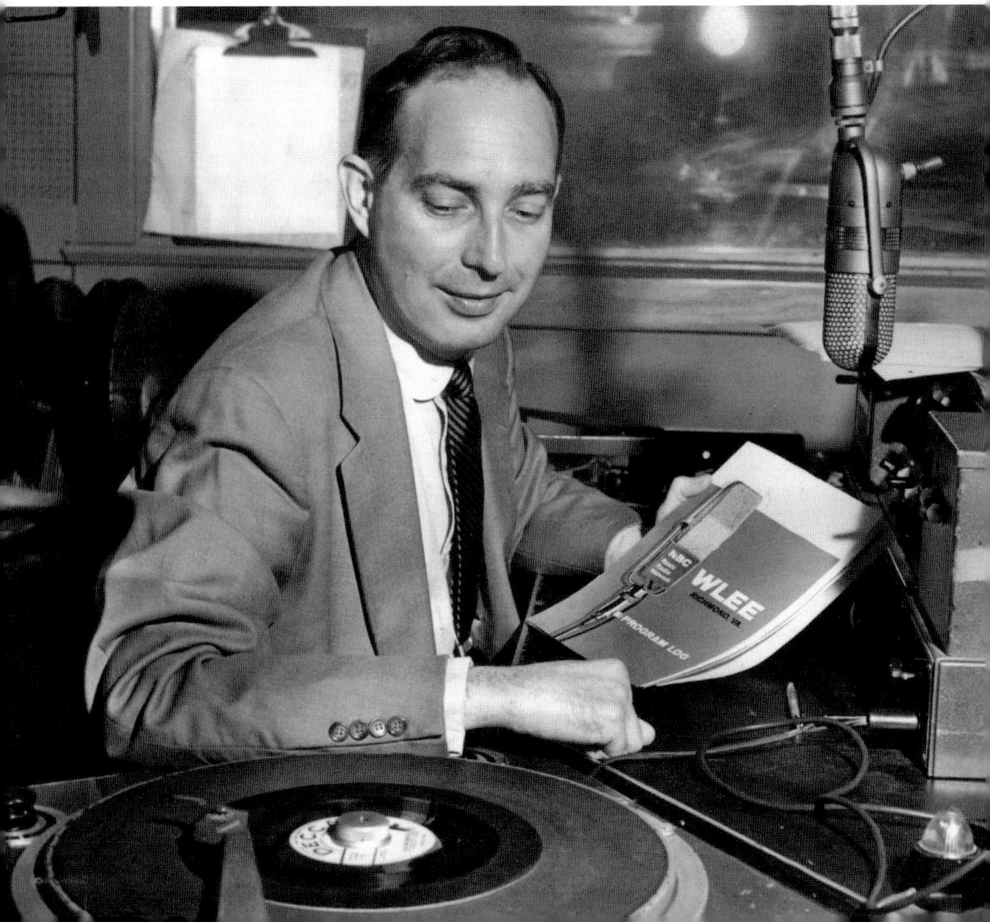

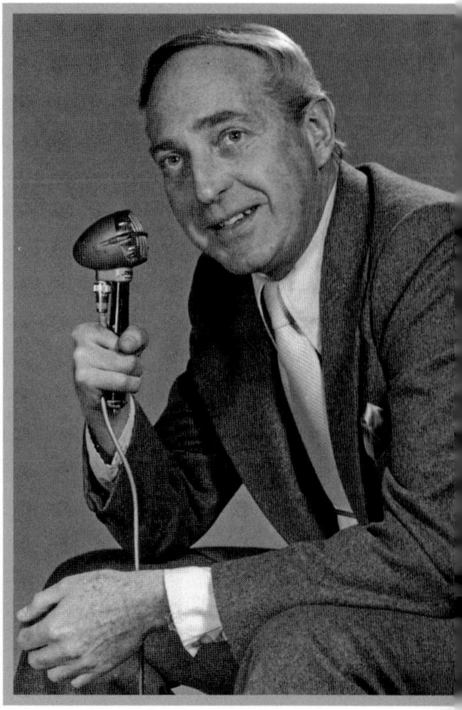

Harvey was a friend to all. When the famed film star Jo Cotton came to town, Harvey did more than just emcee his appearance at the Loew's. He talked Cotton through an unexpected bout of off-screen jitters. "You don't understand." Cotton pleaded. "I don't do this. When I'm on screen, I'm playing someone else. But now, you're expecting *me* to be *me* on stage. I'm terrified!" Harvey counseled him through it, and the show went on. Another time, the great theatre organist Eddie Weaver found himself in a bit of a bind. His console rose to the stage and kept rising, all the way up to the top balcony. "What am I doing here?" Weaver cried. Ol' Harvey leapt to the cause, shutting down the theatre and calling for a fireman to help his friend down.

Harvey is still at it today, nearly 70 years after his first radio appearance. His Passing Parade is a tender mix of old times, and places, and music. And Harvey, well Harvey becomes larger than life with each passing day. He often says that people don't laugh enough. And if you are lucky enough to pass a few minutes with him, you will come to understand that this is not because life is free from conflict, or suffering, or sorrow, but rather, because a little comedy is good for the soul. Here's to you, old friend.

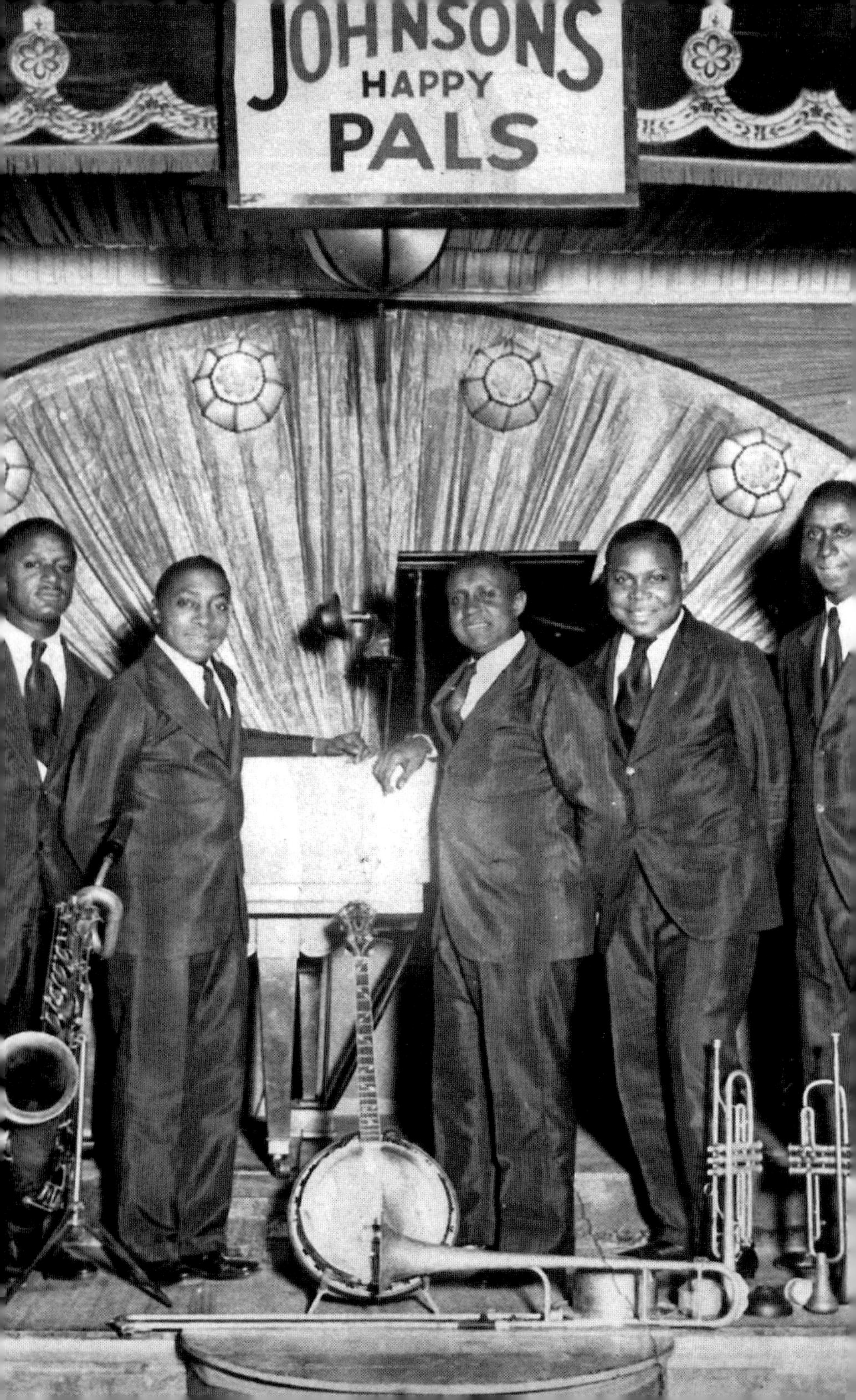
JOHNSONS
HAPPY
PALS

Johnson's Happy Pals

On August 15, 1929, the new world was whirring and spinning wildly into the still imperceptible final throes of the roaring twenties. In New York, the stock market opened to a rallying, "wild bull" rampage. In Chicago, the notorious gangster, Baby Face Nelson, stumbled into justice for neither the first nor the last time. And in Richmond, ten big band jazzmen known as Johnson's Happy Pals walked into a recording studio and lay down the best two tracks you've never heard.

Just a few months later, the world came unhinged. On October 19, in the face of brisk but fleeting recovery, stocks declined in a last minute "storm of selling." By October 24, the selling had reached "near panic proportions." And by October 29, there was nothing near about it, just downright panic.

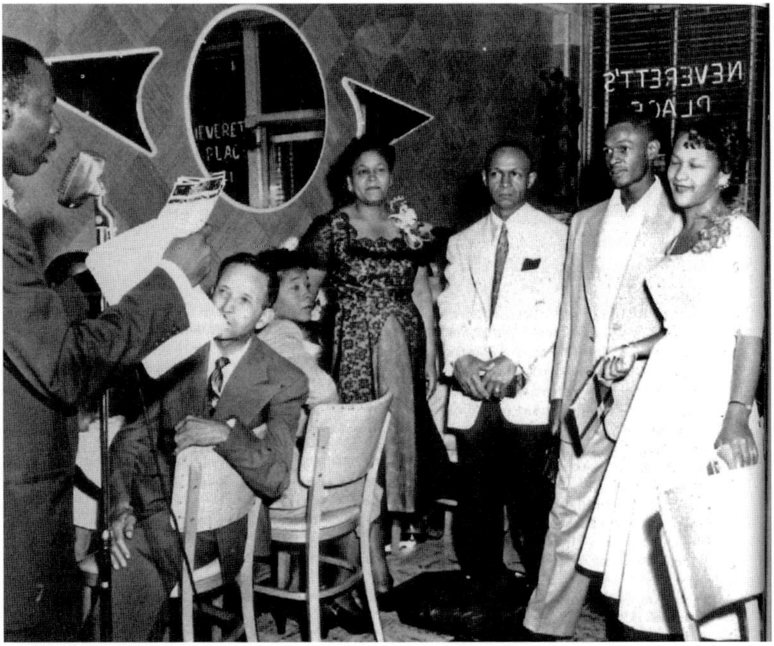

A scene from Neverett's Place, which was one of the many fine jazz clubs in Jackson Ward.

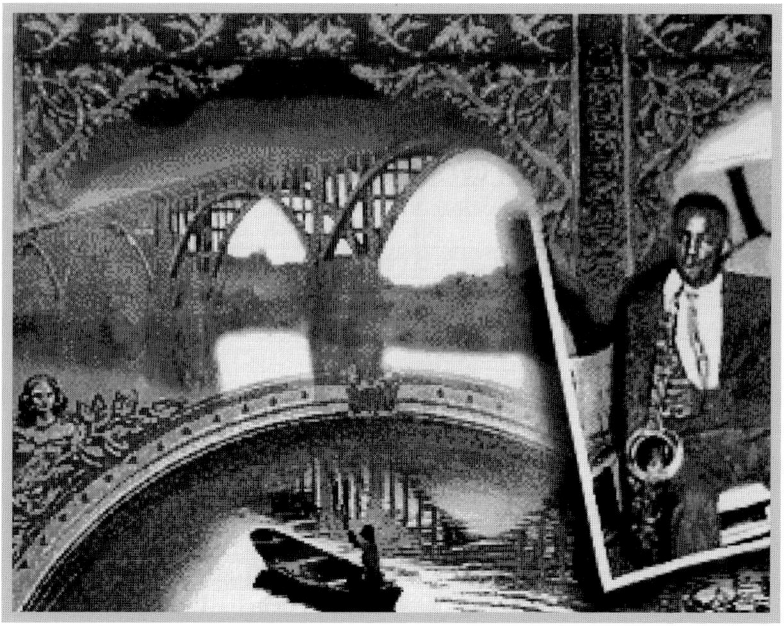

Mosaic art on building at intersection on 3rd and Leigh Streets.

But even in the face of a world teetering off its orbit, Richmond rumbled forward. Our tobacco helped smooth the collective jag. And our rayon replaced blue silk stockings at the society ball. On October 30, in the midst of the greatest financial crash in new world history, the Hotel John Marshall opened its doors. Heralded as the "finest hotel in the south," the John Marshall had radio outlets and circulating ice water in every room. No wonder the *News Leader* was inspired to predict a spectacular recovery in the market just a day later.

Not 300 miles away, the Savoy Ballroom in Harlem was a' titter with happy feet. After all, the Savoy gave us the lindy hop, the jitterbug, and the hint of swing. The Savoy also gave us the most feverish cutting sessions in the country. Dubbed the "battle of the bands," these cutting sessions would pit the greatest jazzmen of the day against one another for all love and glory.

And into this fever strolled our very own Johnson's Happy Pals. They faced Duke Ellington, Fletcher Henderson, and the formidable Chick Webb Orchestra. Guess what? They won.

The Happy Pals continued to play through the ever-imperfect years of Prohibition and the long-sustained Depression. They played rooftop dance halls in Richmond and clubs up and down the east coast. They earned the reputation of inestimable character. They were our premier jazz band.

They are nearly forgotten now, these names from the past: Percy Trent; Slim Harris; Ed "Pickles" Humes; Fred "Floorshow" Culley; Roy Johnson; and others too, a signal mark just to sit in or play through. Alas, there is no plaque or statue, barely a photo of our Pals in their prime. But worry not, sometimes you just have to close your eyes and improvise.

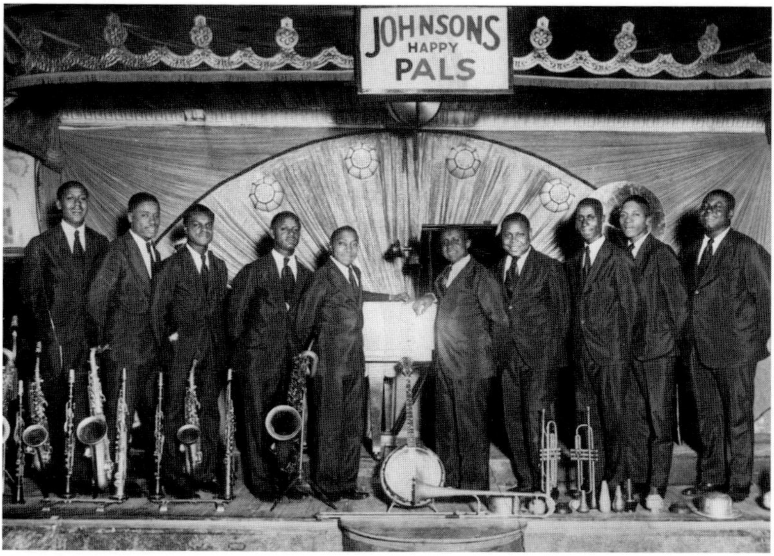

Johnson's Happy Pals at the Savoy Ballroom in New York City, 1929 (Richmond Jazz Society Special Collection).

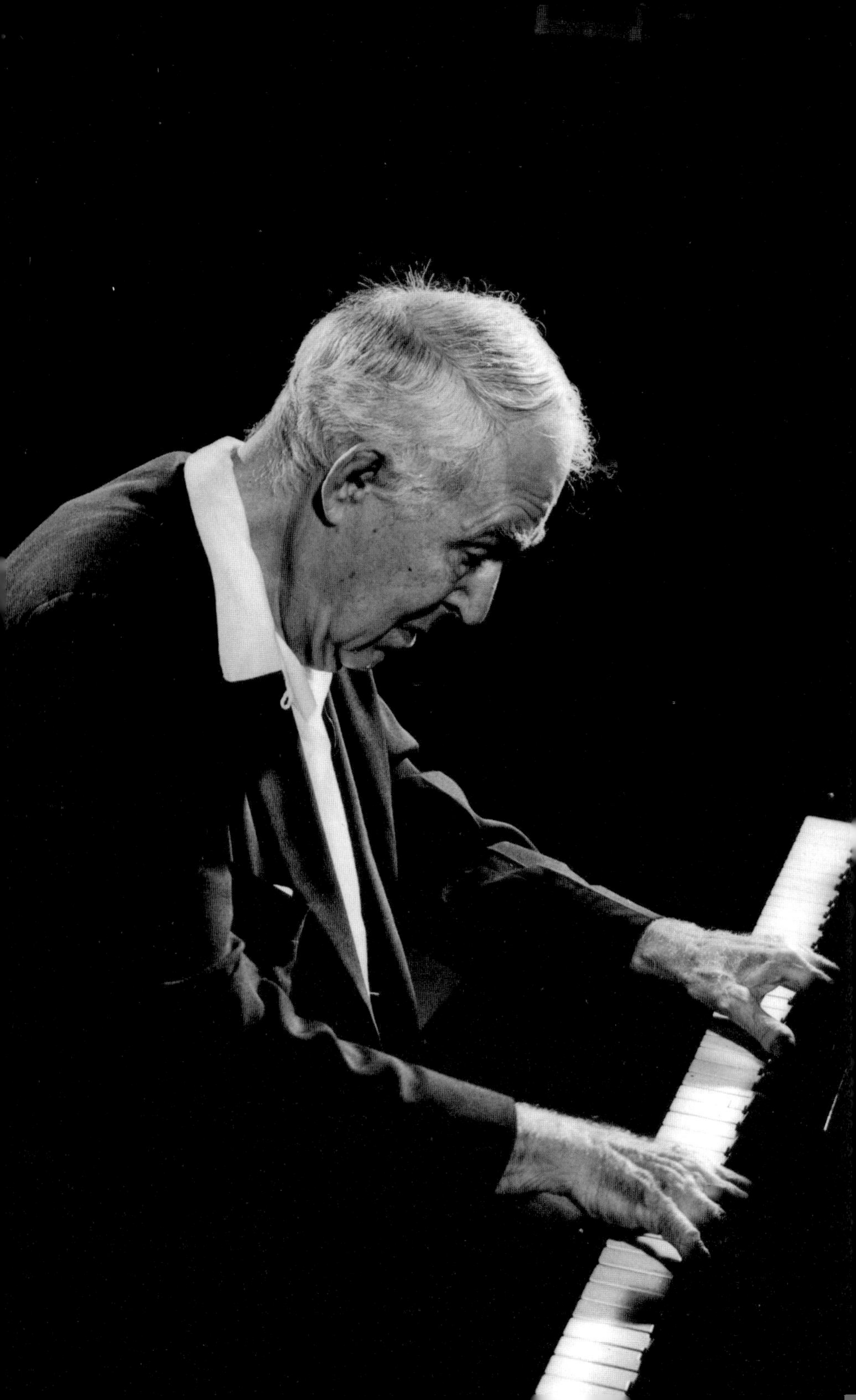

Artists of Plum

Much has been made of the folk movement that ignited Greenwich Village in the 1960s, but did you know that Richmond had its own folk revival and "teensy, tiny" Greenwich Village way back in the 1920s? To be sure, our Village was smaller, more row than *rue boheme*. Helena Caperton described the row in 1929 as "just those two precious blocks [on Plum Street] which Art, whimsical, wayward and without reason, [had] chosen for her home."

Louise Burleigh was the first to take up artist's residence on Plum. The young Miss Burleigh was a playwright, dramatist, and author from New York who moved to Richmond in 1918 to direct the Little Theatre League.

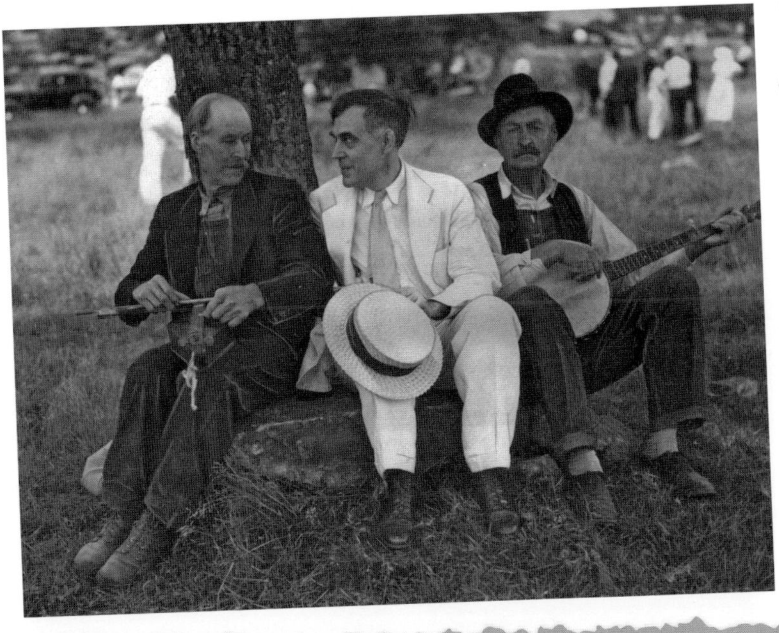

John Powell with colleagues at the White Top Music Festival.

She was soon joined by John Powell, the internationally acclaimed pianist and composer. Powell perfected his first original piano composition at the age of three, and by twelve, was capable of writing six sonatas at once. Powell and Burleigh married in 1928 and made their home at 106 North Plum.

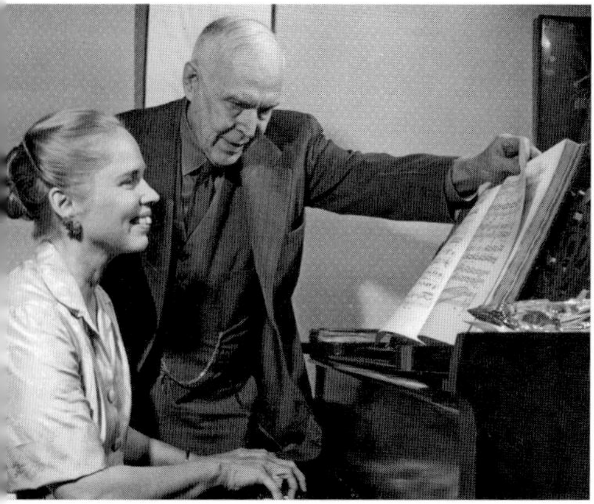

Florence Robertson Givens and John Powell.

Around this time, the Powells welcomed an out-of-town visitor, George Harris, Jr. Harris was a singing tenor and composer, and he was smitten by the Powell's little artist's retreat. Just a few weeks later, he took up residence at 102 North Plum, overcoming certain obvious space constraints by knocking out all of the downstairs walls to make room for his concert grand piano. Harris helped to form the Richmond Symphony Orchestra in 1932, became head of the VCU music department in 1950, and was a long-time music critic for the *Times-Dispatch*.

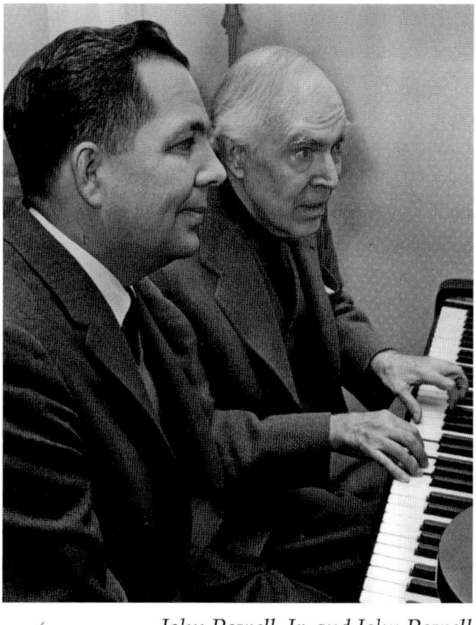

John Powell, Jr. and John Powell.

Both Powell and Harris were enraptured by Appalachian folk music, and they clung to these

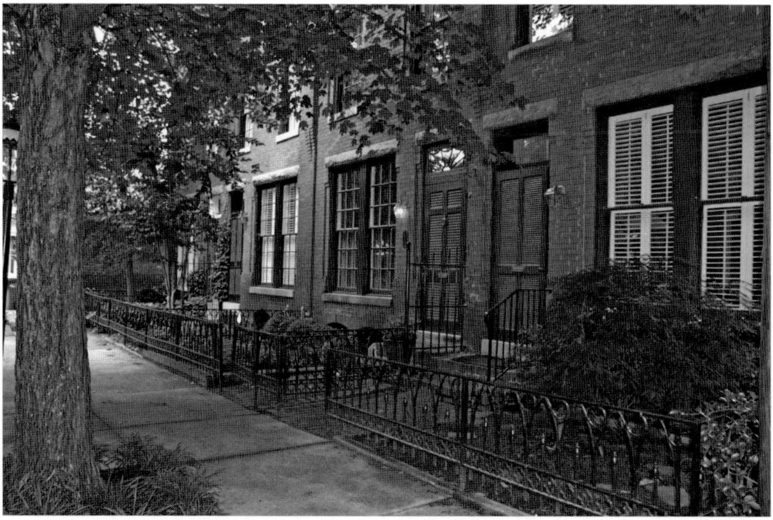

John Powell's residence, 106 N.Plum Street.

old-timey hymns as "soil for the growth of a great school of American music." Louise inspired her husband to draw these hymns into his compositions, and he soon became known the world over for them. As the *London Standard* reported after one Powell performance, "[s]uch charm of vision and execution, such burning eloquence and tender sentiment, such vivid imagination have seldom been crowded into a sitting at the piano."

The Powells left Richmond for the mountains of Albemarle County in the 1930s. But in 1936, a group of admirers banded together to purchase and set aside 106 North Plum as a lifetime gift to their favorite artists.

And so, music poured from the windows, and revolution danced like a butterfly in the communal garden that formed in the alley behind Plum. It may be a quieter place today, but pause for a moment and you may yet hear the hint of bohemian rhapsody.

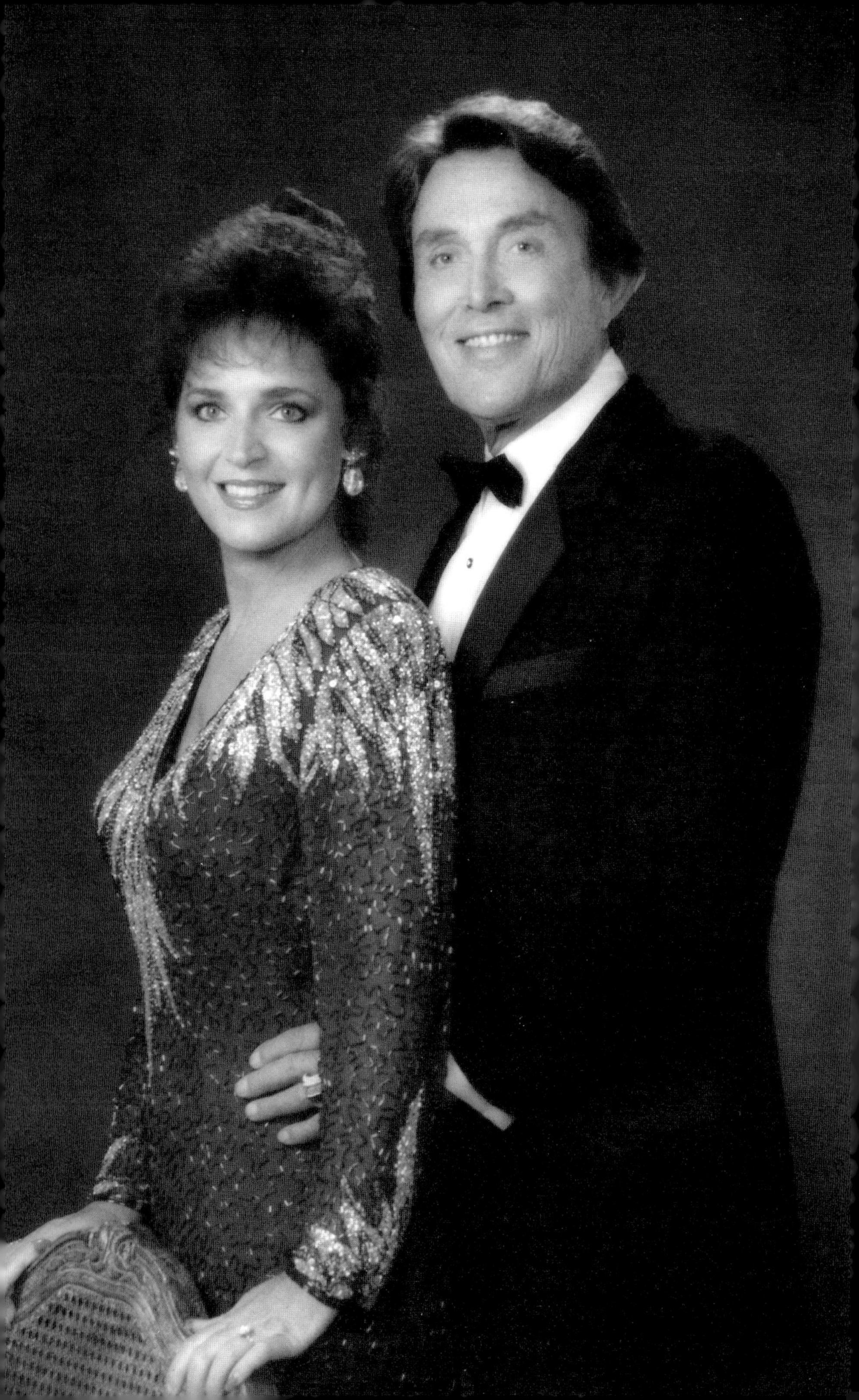

JIMMY DEAN

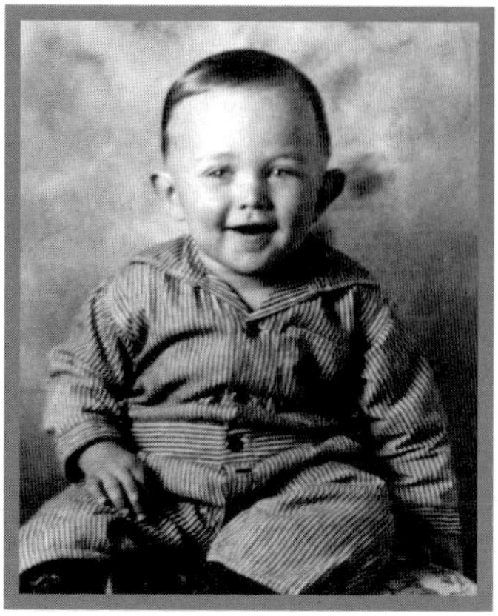
Jimmy Dean's 1-year old portrait.

It is hard to resist the call of the American dream, of the fantastic, nearly impossible beauty that beckons from just a simple ribbon of highway. And though many succumb to the call, few find their way to the dream itself. It is tempting to think that these lucky few are all long gone, products of some happier, more accessible world. But I have on good opinion that at least one of them is still with us. His name is Jimmy Dean, and he lives just down the river from Richmond.

Jimmy's early days were by no means dream-like. In fact, he is fond of saying that the greatest motivating factor in his life was the poverty of his youth. He certainly ran scared from it, imagining that he might one day end up back in Plainview, Texas installing irrigation wells.

As it turns out, Jimmy had little to fear. The arc of his career has been luminous. First in music, then television, then movies and, of course, business too, Jimmy has tasted every sweet morsel of the dream. President Truman enjoyed Jimmy's *Town and Country Time* so much that he used to excuse himself from all affairs of state promptly at 4:30 so that he could watch the show from the quiet of the Oval Office. Jimmy's good friend, Elvis Presley, liked to call him a "country genius S.O.B." And Sean Connery, with whom Jimmy co-starred in the 1971 Bond classic, *Diamonds Are Forever*, referred to

Donna Meade and Jimmy Dean.

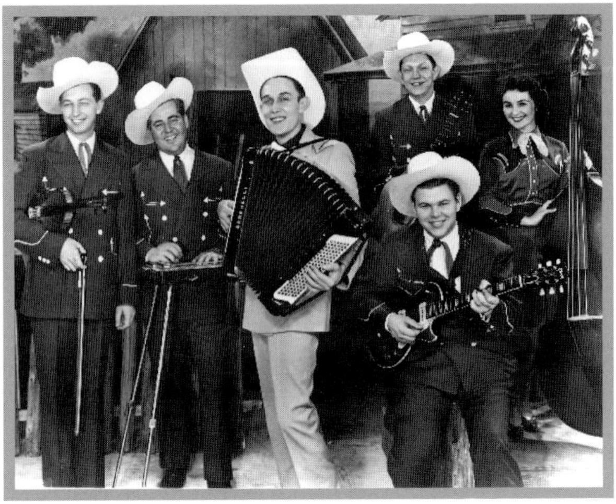

Jimmy Dean with the Texas Wildcats. 1964.

him, affectionately, as that "noisy American."

Jimmy helped to propel more than one rising star to fame. And while many know that he gave Patsy Cline her start, few recall that he did the same for that great muppeteer, Jim Henson. Henson's muppet dog, Rowlf, was a regular on *The Jimmy Dean Show*, and by some accounts, received more fan mail than Jimmy himself.

After a good long run in entertainment, Jimmy shifted his sights to business. With a grin, he'll tell you that if you'd seen his act, you would have appreciated his need for diversification. With a more serious look, he'll tell you that he was still running from the poverty of his youth. His time as "sausage king" is a story in itself; his adventures in banking,

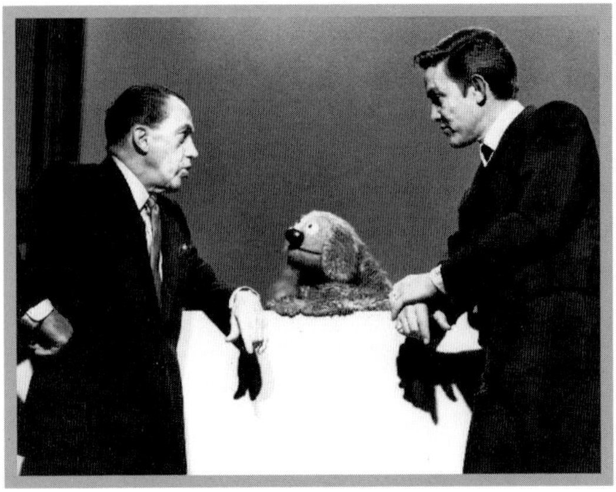

Ed Sullivan and Jimmy Dean with Rowlf, one of Jim Henson's renowned muppets. 1964.

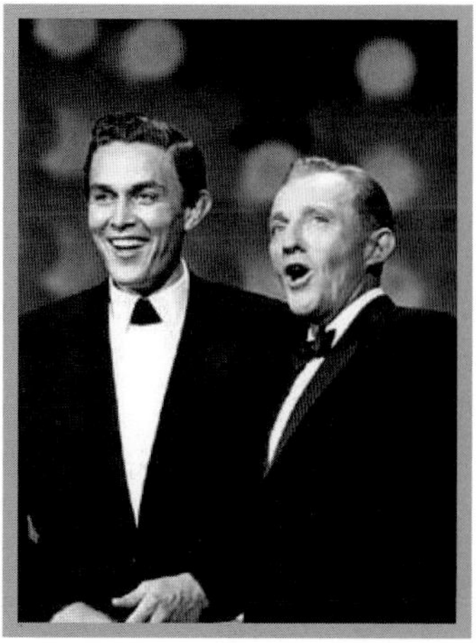

Jimmy Dean with Bing Crosby at the Hollywood Bowl.

limousines, Christmas tree farms, lime groves, restaurants, and race horses are but sidelines in the story.

And just when you thought that the dream could not get any better, Jimmy found both a soul mate and a soulful place. His soul mate is Donna Meade Dean, a true Virginia beauty, an accomplished singer and songwriter, a Miss Richmond finalist, Virginia Female Vocalist of the Year, and new Sunshine Sue in the mid-70's revival of the venerable *Old Dominion Barn Dance.* Jimmy's soulful place is a bluff atop a bend in the mighty James. "An easy place," he calls it. The only place he's ever really lived.

If you get a chance to sit with him as the river rolls by, you will see that Jimmy Dean is not running scared any longer. After all, he has lived the dream *and* lived to tell its two most important lessons: first, wealth and success are just a state of mind; and second, if you don't grin once in a while, you might miss it.

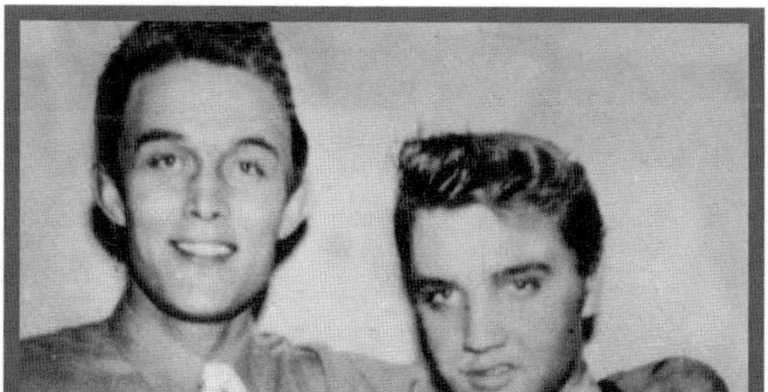

Jimmy Dean and Elvis Presley on WMAL-TV in Washington, D.C. 1956.

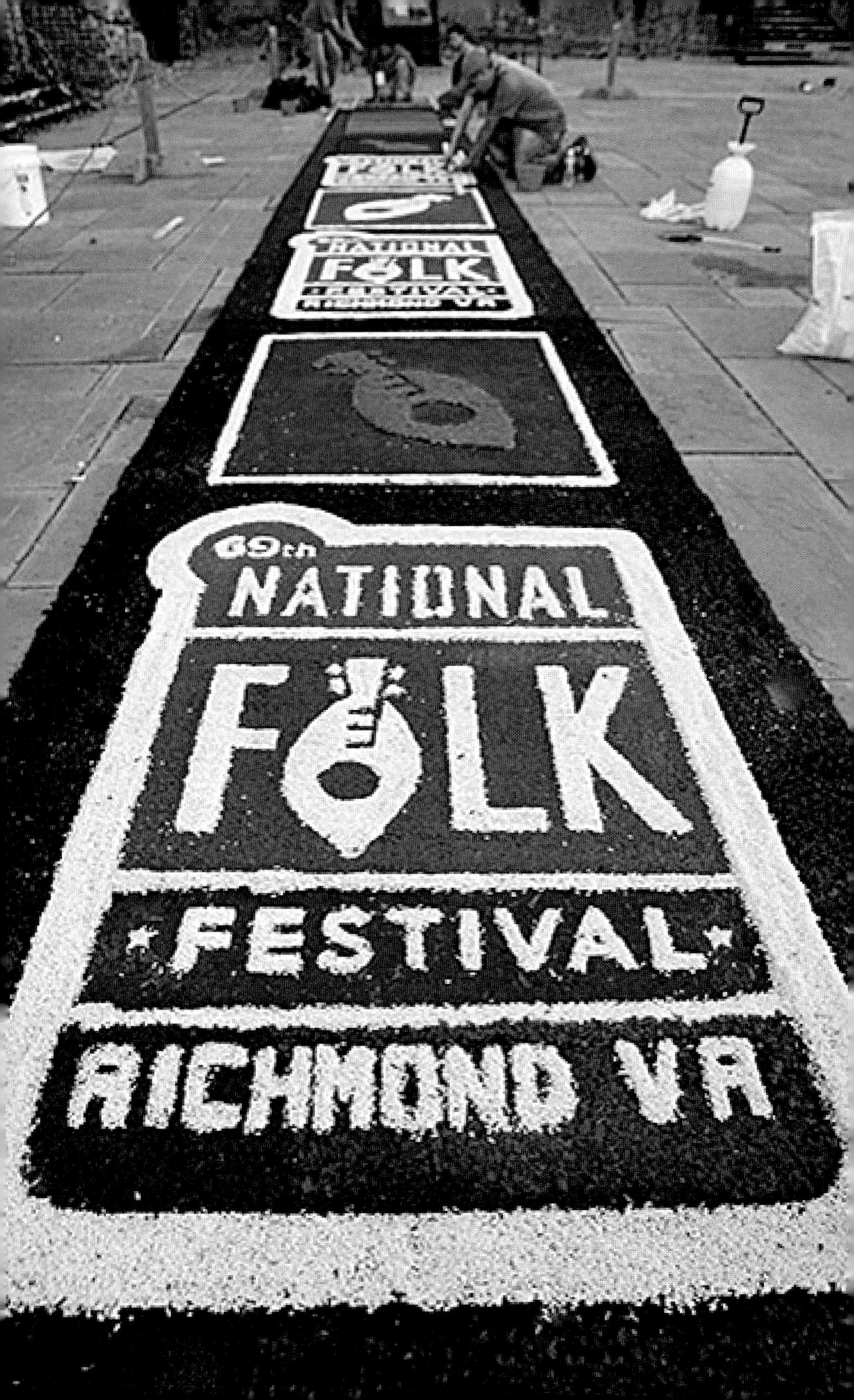
69th
NATIONAL
FOLK
FESTIVAL
RICHMOND VA
NATIONAL
FOLK
FESTIVAL
RICHMOND VA

FOLK FESTIVAL

All this fuss and hustle, this zeal to get ahead,
Each parry a struggle for a taste of daily bread.
Where is the pause, the peace or the grace?
Where do we mend in today's jagged race?

In music, song and dance, I say, our tonic for the soul,
Pray drop your rock now, by and by, and let it roll, roll, roll.
Follow it down to Tredegar, along the river's way,
And let the crooners sing their souls to lift your woes away.

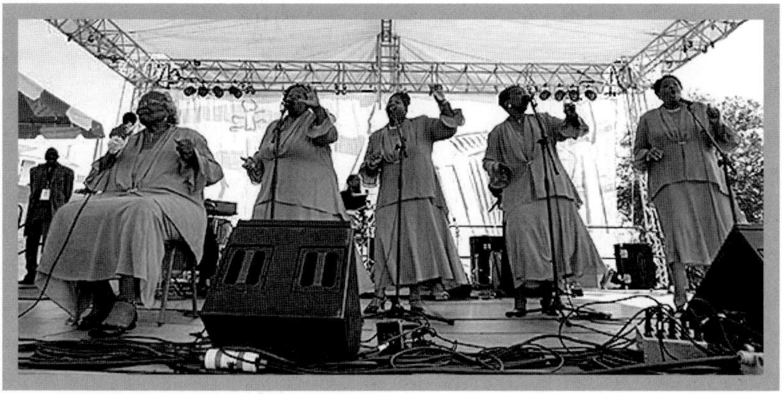

Richmond, Virginia is known as a crossroad for crooked trail bluegrass and tidewater blues, for mountain gospel and lowland shout. But for three rarified days in October, Richmond will transform from passage to promised land.

Where else in the world can you go to find Ethiopian liturgical music, Filipino gong, Persian hammered dulcimer, tamburitza, marimba, funk, zydeco, Latin dance, gospel, honky-tonk, Cajun blues,

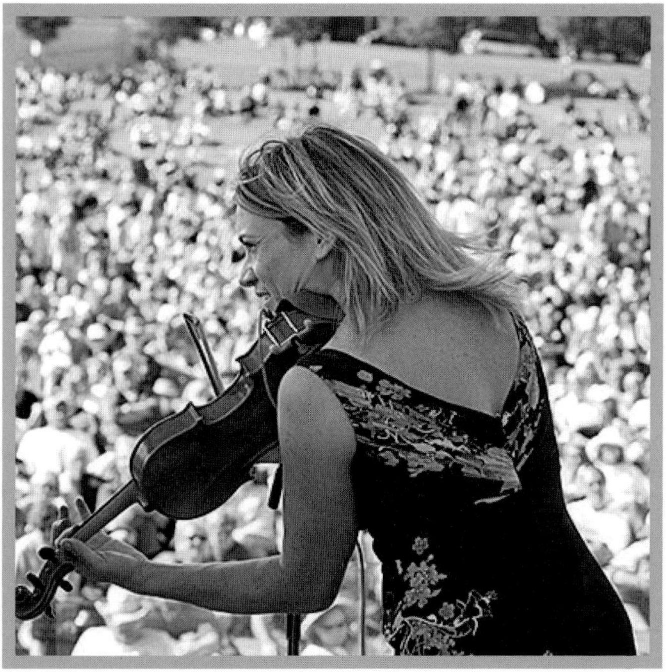

R&B, and claw-handed banjo, all in one place? Fiddles and drums, spoons and washboards stacked like driftwood on the banks of America's founding river.

And in this tangled mass of musical firmaments, perhaps a common thread? A simple excess, an aspiration – the unexpected high note, blown or sung or thumbed as if to pitch us all over the top, suspended in mad frolic, all the sadness and suffering of the world removed, if only for a moment.

In 1968, the famed French sailor, Bernard Moitessier, fussed and hustled into the lead of the first, continuous around-the-world yacht race. But instead of claiming his certain prize, he veered unexpectedly off-course, abandoning both his lead and the race. He left behind a note that read: "I am continuing non-stop toward the Pacific Islands because I am happy at sea, and perhaps also to save my soul."

Well, I am happy in music, and under the tents of the 69th National Folk Festival, among mixed colors, cultures, ages, and genres, down along the banks of the James River in Richmond, I may yet hear a note that will save my soul. The gates open at 6 p.m. on October 12th, and regardless of finish line, far or near, I hope you'll join me.

Author's note: This essay was penned in celebration of the 69th National Folk Festival in October 2007. After hosting the national event for three years, Richmond took the reigns for its very own Richmond Folk Festival in 2008. With any luck, the festival will serve as a centerpiece of music in our fair City for many years to come.

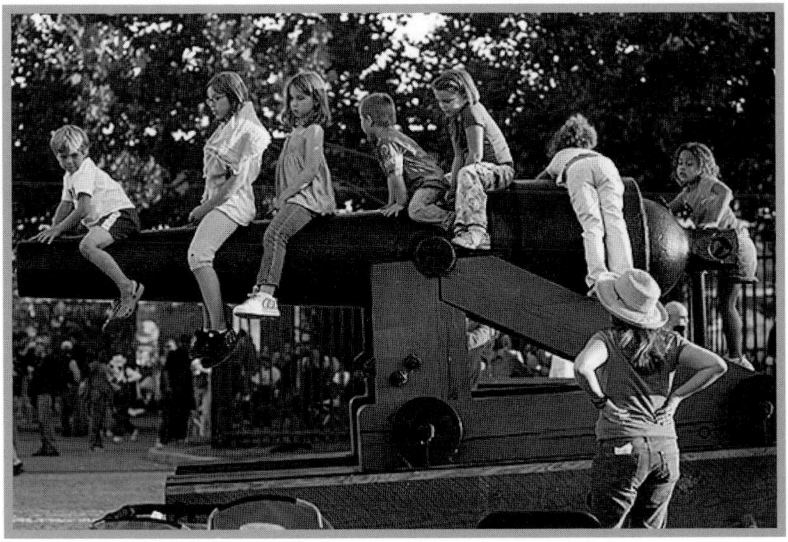

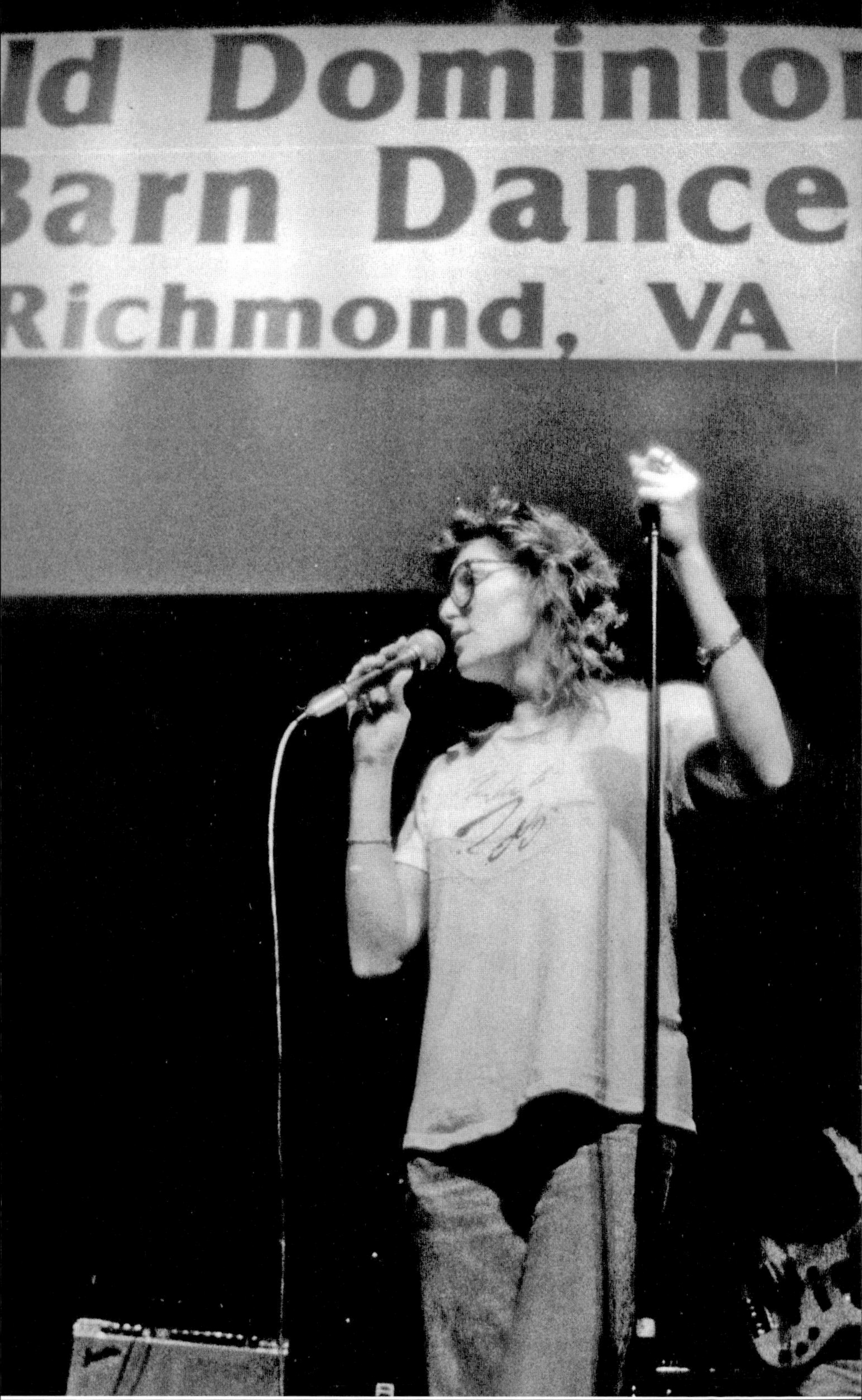

ld Dominio
Barn Dance
Richmond, VA

Old Dominion Barn Dance

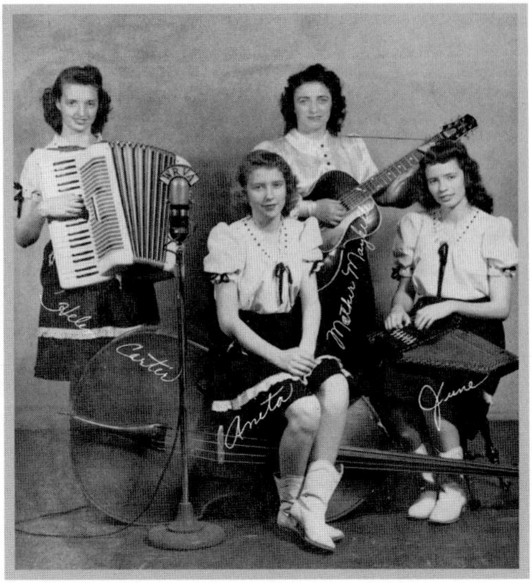

Maybelle, Mother of the three Carter Sisters – Helen, June and Anita. June Carter went on to marry Johnny Cash. The girls were all born in Scott County, Virginia.

On September 14, 1946, WRVA launched the *Old Dominion Barn Dance*, a rambunctious, foot-stomping, old-timey review that was broadcast live from the Lyric Theatre every Saturday night. *The Barn Dance* became a blockbuster with sell-out shows, loyal listeners from sea to shining sea, and a fan base rivaling that of the *Grand Ole Opry* in Nashville. By the 1950s, our *Barn Dance* was reported to be "one of the Commonwealth's chief claims to fame."

The show featured the Carter Sisters, Grandpa Jones, the Saddle Sweethearts, Crazy Joe Maphis, and Mrs. John Workman, better known as Sunshine Sue. Sue was considered to be the heart, brains, and beauty of the *Old Dominion Barn Dance*. A "drawling songstress and mistress of ceremonies," she was crowned "Hillbilly Queen" of all Virginny by Governor Tuck in 1949.

Sunshine Sue attracted all manner of celebrities to the show, including Lester Flatt and Earl Scruggs in 1954, and even the King

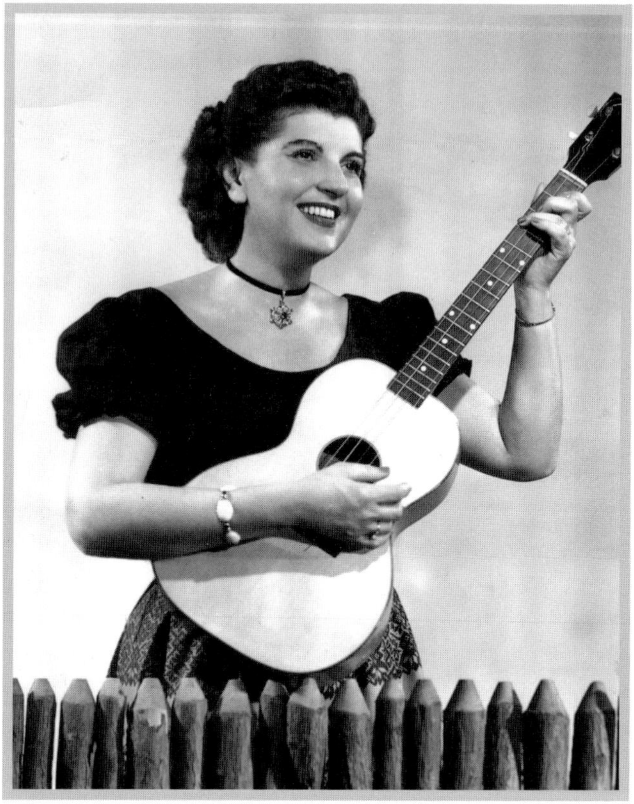

Sunshine Sue.

– Elvis Presley, that is – in 1955. Though Lester and Earl stayed on for months, Elvis' visit was cut short, apparently because Sue did not believe that the gyrating young rock-and-roller fit the family-style atmosphere of the *Old Dominion Barn Dance*.

Sunshine Sue's show was by no means just a southern phenomenon. In the mid-50s, the *Old Dominion Barn Dance* traveled to New York City for a three-week off-Broadway engagement that proved to be a wildly popular, sell-out success. Just imagine, hillbillies in New York!

Sadly, the show faded from the scene in 1957, and Sunshine Sue

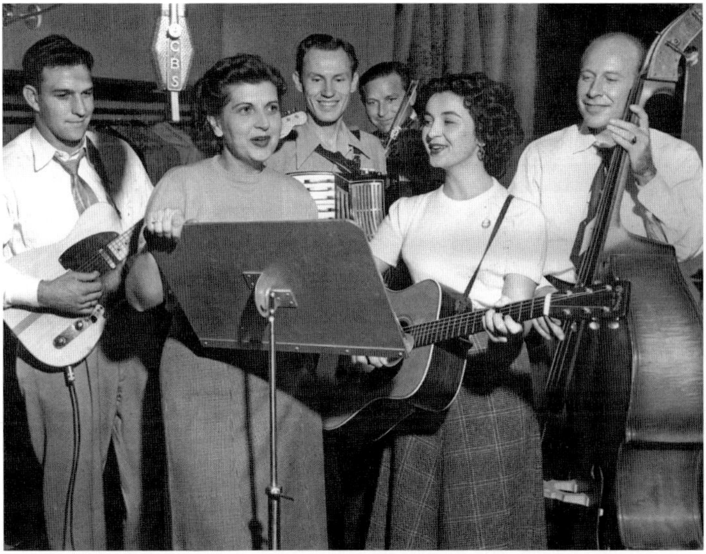

Sunshine Sue and members of the Old Dominion Barn Dance band.

passed away at the all-too-early age of 67. Nostalgia for the show inspired a revival in 1973 at the State Fairgrounds, and again in 1991 at the Carpenter Center. But the new *Barn Dance* was never quite the same as the old one. After all, the times had changed.

Sunshine Sue was once asked why hillbilly music had become so popular. She responded: "There's a yearning to get back to unpaved soil and uncomplicated living. Our kind of music is so simple, soothing, reassuring, and direct that people just can't seem to get along without it."

Well, the times may have changed, but that old yearning has not. Sunshine Sue, we miss you.

Author's Note: No story about the Old Dominion Barn Dance is complete without tipping a hat at its successor, the New Dominion Barn Dance. This reincarnation featured "The Country Cavaliers," an award-winning house band that also hosted a television show on Channel 8 every Sunday for many years. Though the new review did not have Sunshine Sue, it did have its share of visiting celebrities, including Johnny Cash, Ray Price, Buck Owens, and Little Jimmy Dickens.

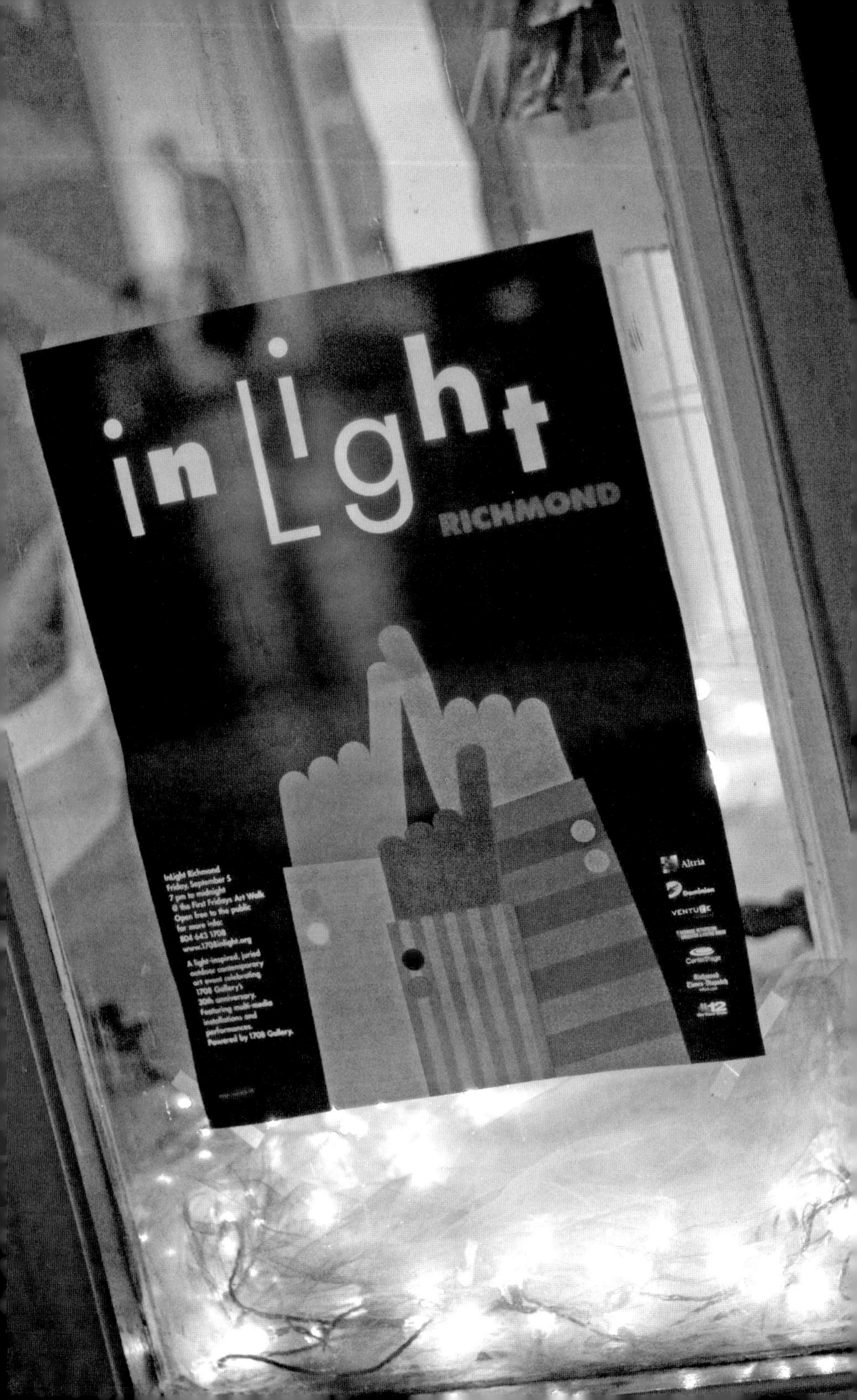

inLight
RICHMOND
InLight Richmond
Friday, September 5
7 pm to midnight
@ the First Fridays Art Walk
Open free to the public
for more info:
804 643 1708
www.1708inlight.org
A light-inspired, juried outdoor contemporary art event celebrating 1708 Gallery's 30th anniversary. Featuring multi-media installations and performances. Powered by 1708 Gallery.

InLight Richmond

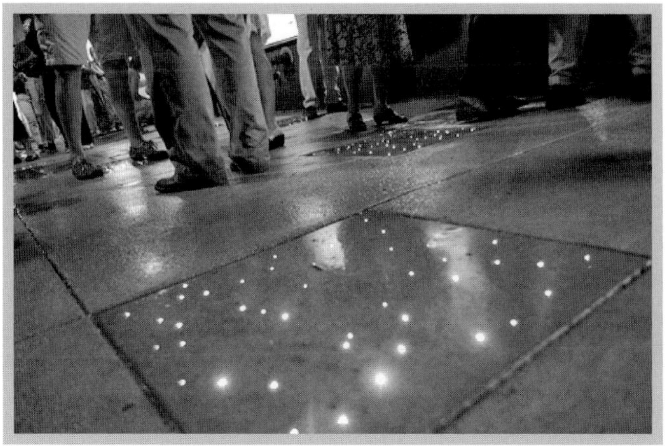

Oh light diffuse around my bed,
To warm my eyes and right my head,
To draw me up and out the door,
In search of tones not seen before.

Oh fading light my heart's dismay,
To see but another end to day,
To leave the canvas and brushes wet,
The scene undone or not done yet.

Oh smite the bellows and loose the flame,
Tempt light from darkness and pray reclaim,
That dazzling vision of the mind's eye,
To sing and paint until it's dry.

At 8 p.m. on Friday, September 8, 1978, twenty-one artists unleashed 1708 Gallery, a "bold new experiment" in Richmond, an "alternative space" for art and artists with the singular

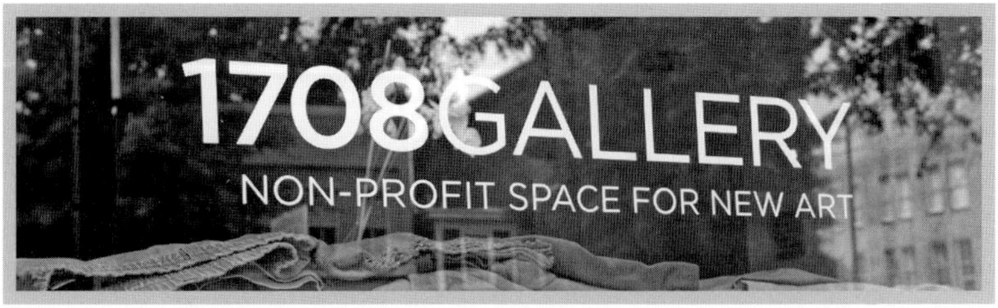

purpose of "filling the gap between what museums are able to do for contemporary art, what the artists themselves need, and what the public deserves to see." With initial funding from the National Endowment for the Arts, 1708 committed itself, its space, its artists, and its ideas to expanding the understanding, development, and appreciation of contemporary art.

And while no start-up is certain of success, least of all an experimental one, 1708 flourished. It survived the flood of 1985,

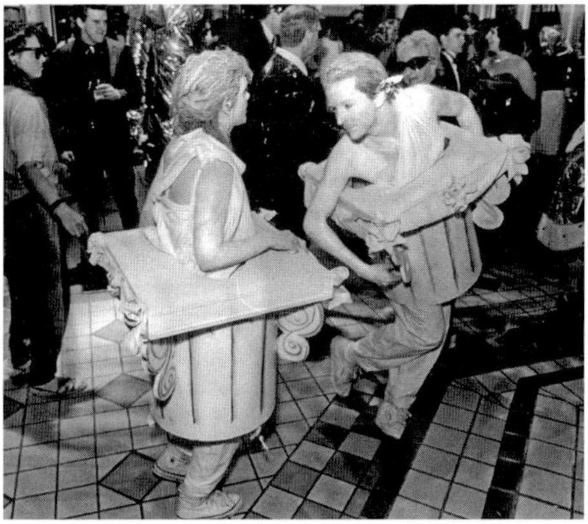

which poured 8 feet of water into the gallery's first home; the censorship battle of 1990, which pitted the City against 1708 in a rancorous First Amendment case; two moves; countless critics; and a mass of humanity distracted at every turn by the papal dogmas of the quattrocento, which is to say, convention.

Without question, 1708 helped to break down these dogmas. In 1985, it invited us to "step into our favorite work of art" for its landmark Beaux Arts Ball. Just imagine a room filled with revelers

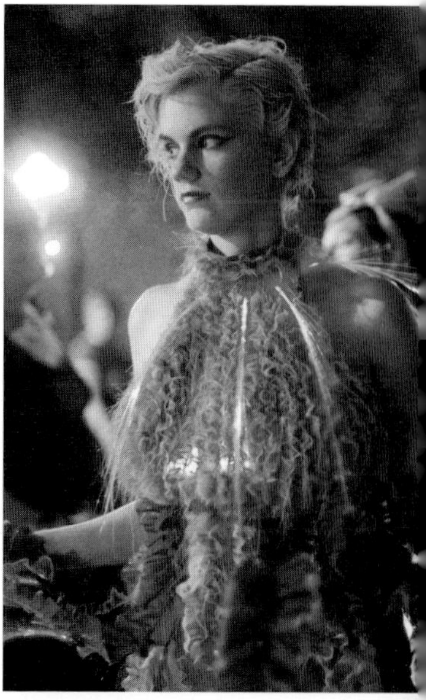

dressed as the couple in Grant Wood's *American Gothic*, or the shattered soul in Munch's *The Scream*, or a Fabergé Egg. Over the years, 1708 gave us colossal masks, urbicultural demonstrations, installations of every shape and hue, artists without borders, paintings without paint, and even mind over matter.

On September 8, 2008, our alternative space turned thirty. We celebrated this milestone with InLight Richmond, the newest bold experiment from our beloved alternative space. InLight transformed Broad Street into our collective canvas, illuminated by light-inspired installations from around the globe, and decked by roving dancers, musicians, and untold thousands of Richmonders willing to add their own lighted bodies and brushes to the experiment.

Come, let us celebrate this remarkable space. Let us sing and paint, smite the bellows and loose the flame, and tempt light from darkness as 1708 has taught us to do.

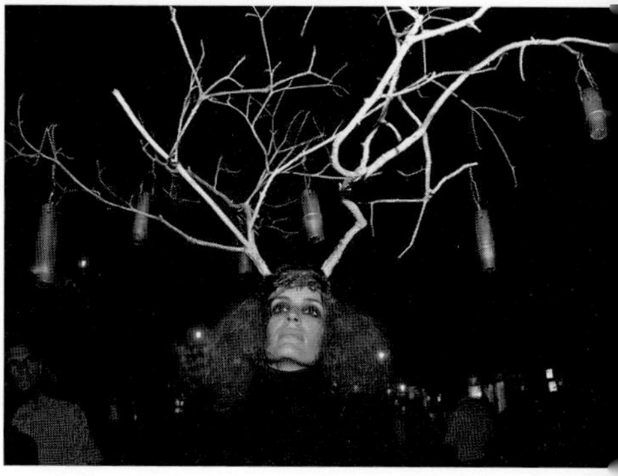

Author's Note: This essay was inspired by, and dedicated to, the inaugural InLight celebration. Fortunately for Richmond, the embers from this celebration continue to burn bright. A second InLight celebration is planned for late September 2009, when the downtown arts and entertainment district will once again be transformed by artists wielding white hot light.

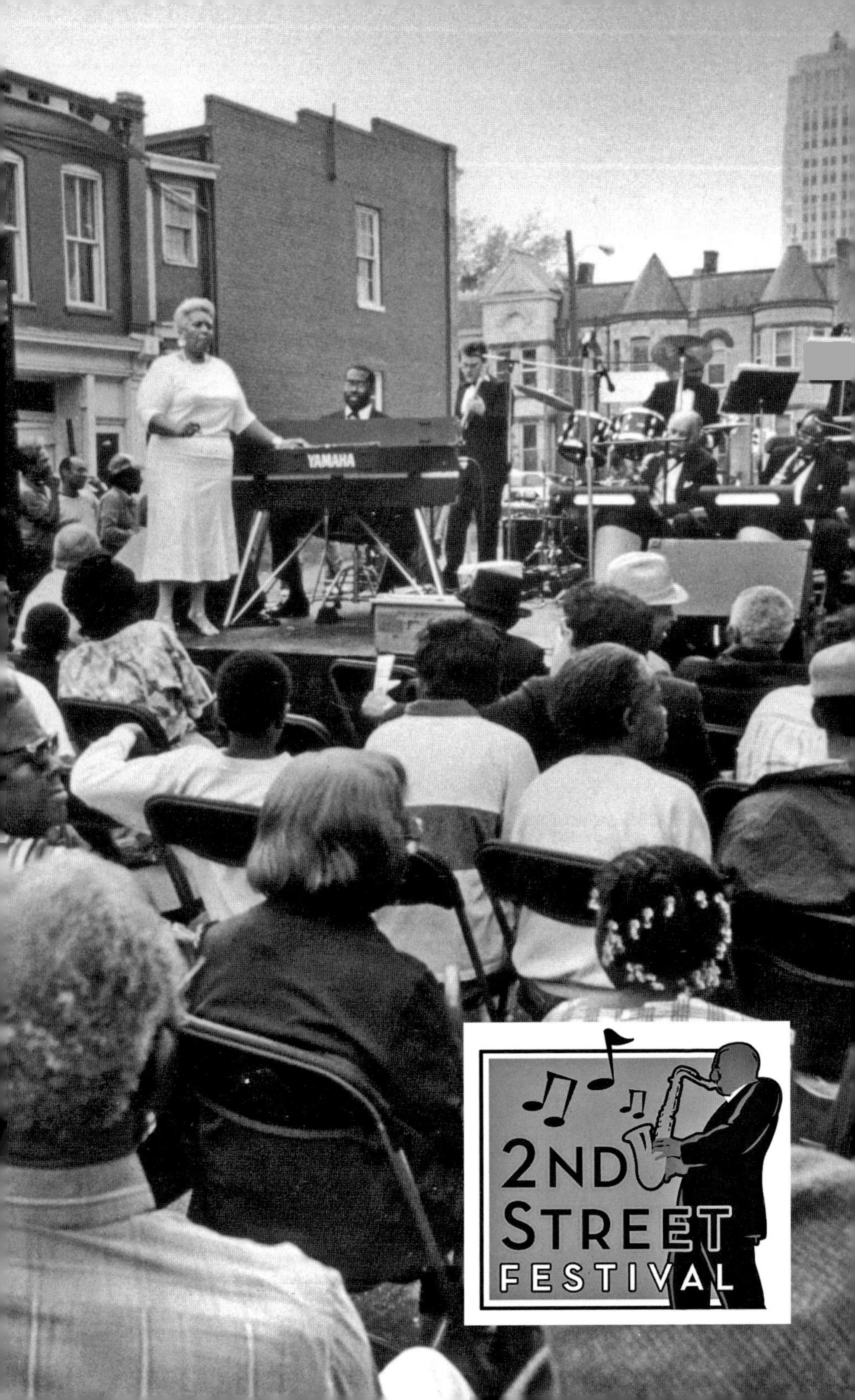
YAMAHA
2ND
STREET
FESTIVAL

2nd Street Festival

Twenty years ago, the Black History Museum, Richmond Renaissance, and the Valentine History Center collaborated on a short documentary about 2nd Street as it was back in the day – about the Deuce, the old red heart of black Richmond. At the time, 2nd Street was suffering the dual slights of inattention and urban decay. Some participants saw the documentary as a way of giving the Deuce a decent burial. But who could have known that it would help to spark her rebirth?

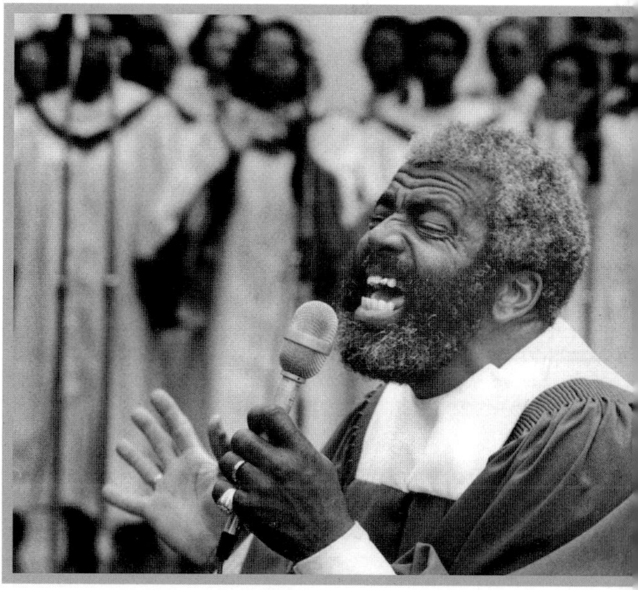

When the documentary was released in 1989, the collaborators organized a community celebration that conjured up the vitality of a bygone day. This celebration inspired the 2nd Street Festival, which has been running ever since. For one weekend each October, 2nd Street overflows with music, storytelling, antique cars, home cooking and people, throngs of them, up to 80,000 strong by some accounts, all reunited like one big family splintered by time and circumstance.

To be fair, 2nd Street enjoyed more than a bygone day. For decades, from the roaring twenties to the war-torn forties and beyond, the Deuce was an oasis of black commerce and entertainment. It teemed with restaurants, movie houses, markets, hotels, lawyers, doctors, florists, and banks. Name it and you could find it along 2nd Street or in the tight, culturally rich Jackson Ward neighborhood that surrounded it.

At Big Al's Shoe Shine Parlor, you could attend to your feet and the latest jazz LPs spinning on Al's phonograph. Down the way at the Polka Dot Club, Tap Turner's Place, or the scores of other nightclubs that dotted the Deuce, you could hear the greatest of the Ward's jazz musicians, from Bongo Buck and Bongo Jim to Guitar Slim, Jay Bird, Boo Gates, Fats Harrison, and Fleming Askew. On Saturday nights, the lines for movies at the Globe and Hippodrome wrapped around all four corners. On Sunday afternoons, the Elks Club hosted parades up and down 2nd Street. And nearly any time of day, you might be lucky

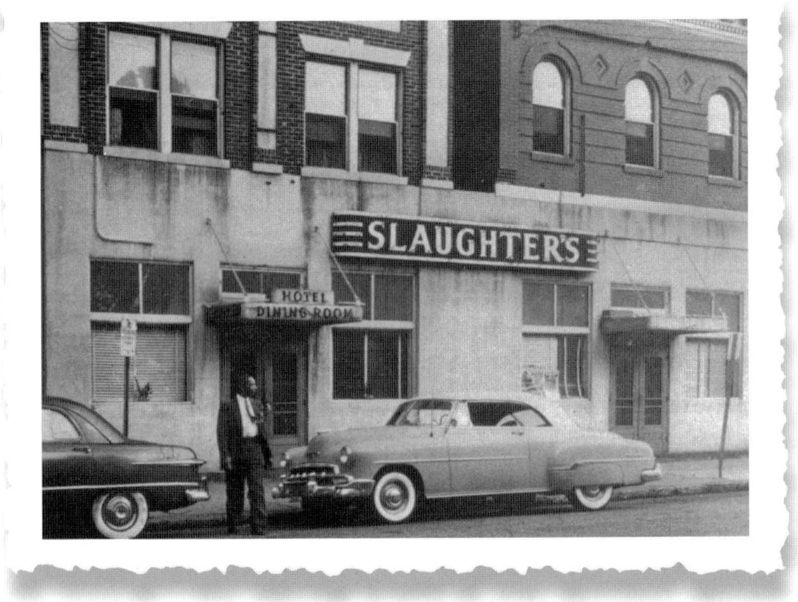

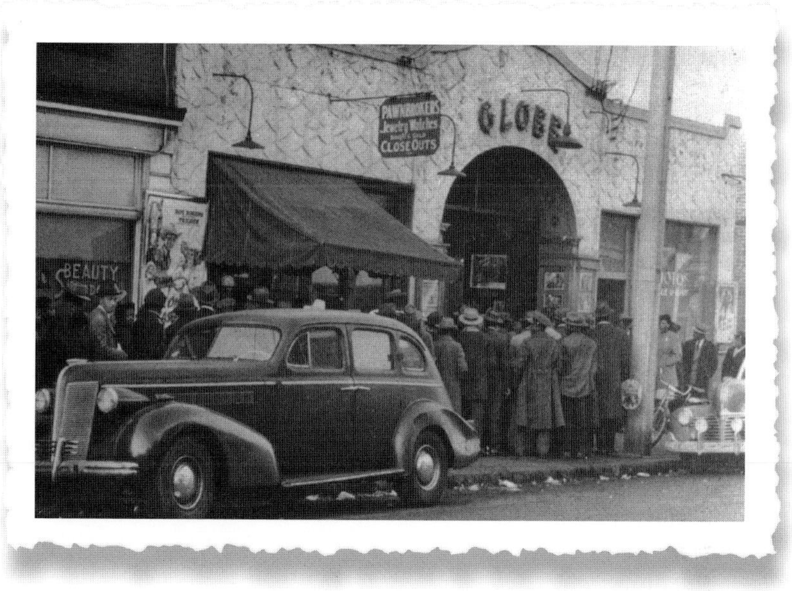

enough to spy Willie Mays or Fighting Joe Louis at the counter of Rosa Brown's.

The Deuce in Jackson Ward is as enigmatic as its host. Some say that the Ward is named for James Jackson, who ran a beer garden at 2nd and Leigh back in the 1820s. Others cite Giles Jackson, the first black person to be admitted to the practice of law by the Supreme Court of Virginia at the turn of the twentieth century, and a leading entrepreneur who helped to establish a newspaper, hotel, home for the elderly, and sundry other businesses to serve the Ward. Whatever the true namesake, the Ward and her Deuce have soulful pedigree.

To *be happy* is a state of mind. To *get happy* takes a little elbow grease. These days, the Deuce is a bit of both. Visit her during the festival this fall and you will see her abloom. But don't wait until then. The old red heart of Richmond beats every day of the year.

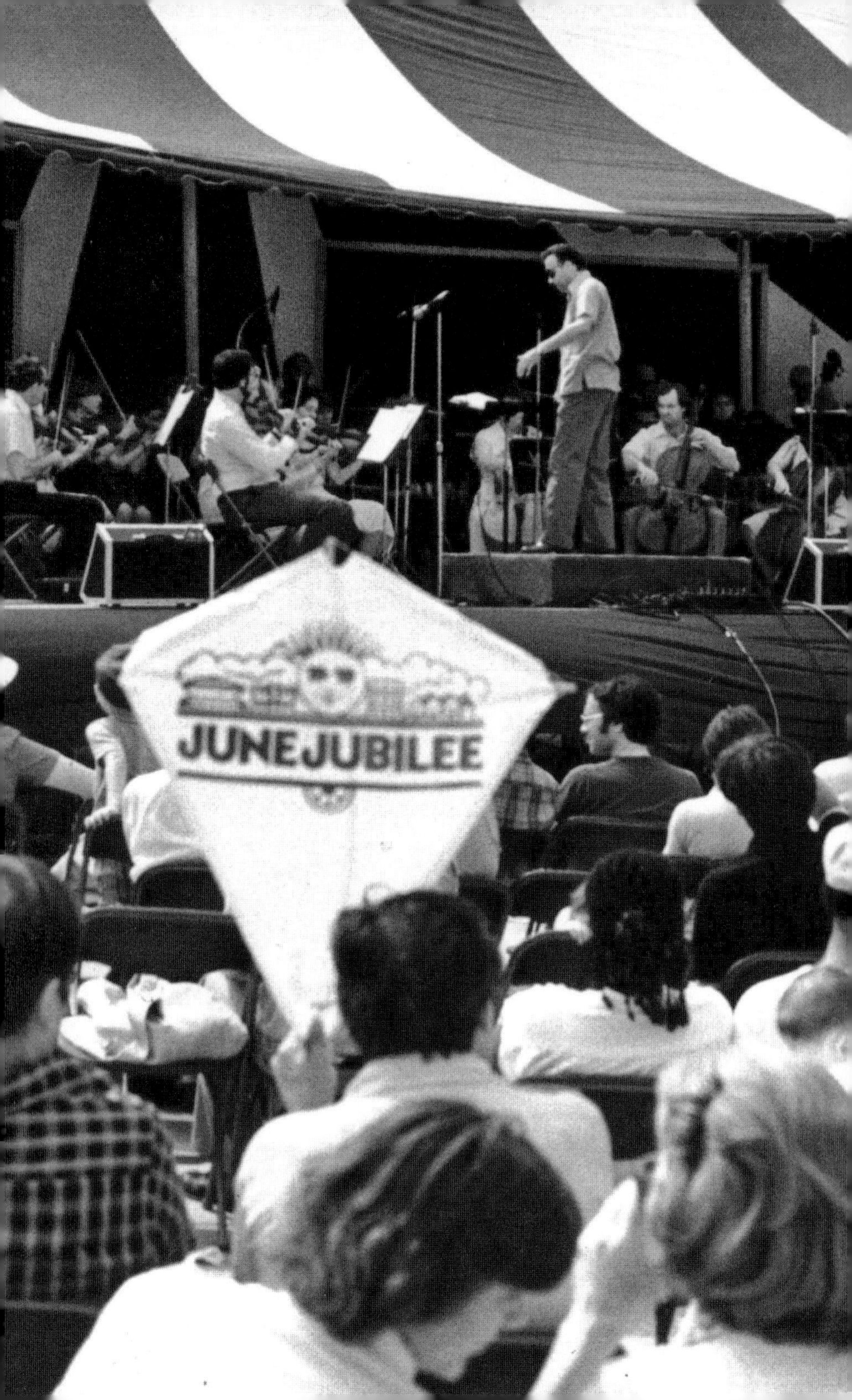
JUNEJUBILEE

JUNE JUBILEE

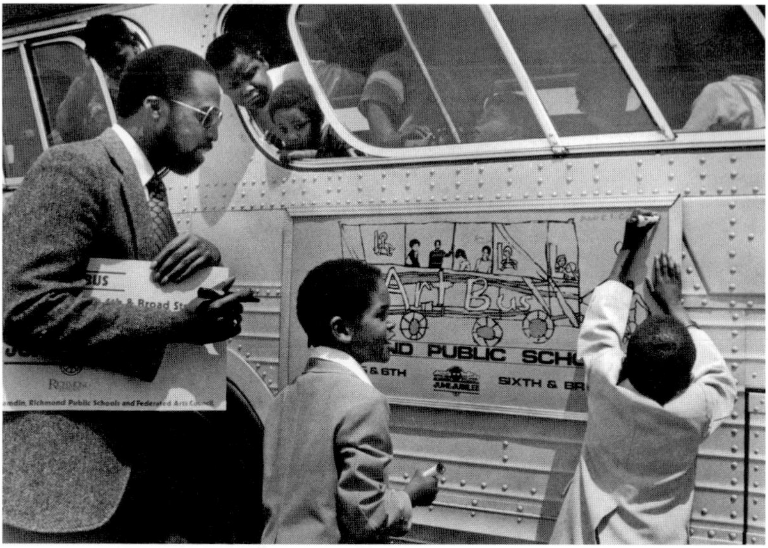

First graders Kimani Brown and Andre Seward sign their work mounted on the side of the Art Bus.

In 1976, some happy dissidents hatched a hare-brained idea, surely characteristic of the emotional haze of the time, to launch an experimental arts festival in downtown Richmond. Their idea was to try to draw people back into the City, to bring us all together through music and dance. Features from this first festival included the Ezibu Muntu Dancers, the Richmond Chapter of the Clowns of America, and a line of buses filled with grade school art. Without question, the festival was a gamble of immense proportions. What if, after all of the hard work and planning, no one showed up?

Well, not to worry. The hare-brained idea proved to be more than passing giddiness. It was pure, creative genius. The first festival drew over 100,000 people in just two days. Within a few years, attendance

◄ *June Jubilee. 1987.*

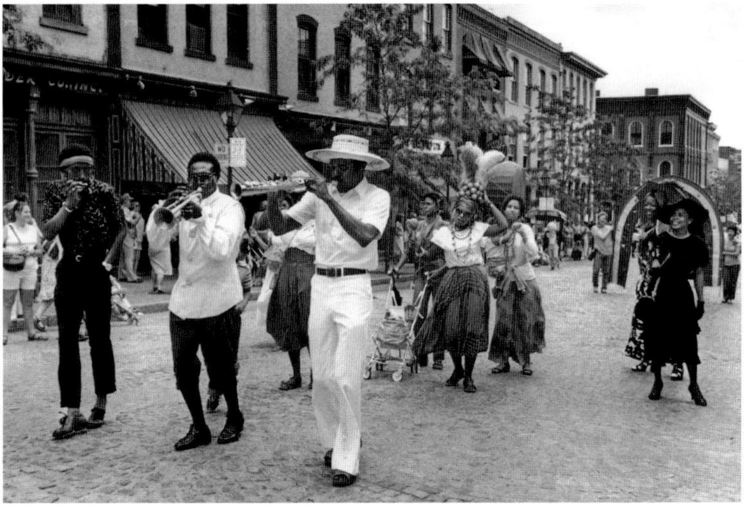

Richmond Jazz Society on parade during June Jubilee, 1981.

doubled. And over a sustained run of 20 years, the festival, known as June Jubilee, consistently drew hundreds of thousands of people back into the City. Its wild success was seen as proof to many that there was indeed a thirst for a downtown performing arts center, a thirst that is just now being quenched, decades later, with the soon-to-open Richmond CenterStage complex.

But June Jubilee was not simply a mechanical hare that paraded metronomically down the streets of the City. It was a little piece of the heart of Richmond writ large. And from time to time, it beat irregularly. In 1988, festival planners believed they were at a turning point as they sought to vault the festival to a more national stage. They even brought in consultants from Seattle's Bumbershoot Festival to help guide their gilded path. But what they ultimately realized was that the event's real draw was the jubilant mix of local people – young and old, black and white, rich and poor. We were not trying to be someone or someplace else. We were just trying to be ourselves. If you wanted to come dressed as a piece of art, you could. If you wanted to blow your horn to everyone and no one, you could do that too.

For many years, June Jubilee was considered the first downtown festival in our fair City. But as I have come to learn, everything in Richmond has a forerunner. On May 14, 1900, some happy dissidents hatched a hare-brained idea to fill Broad Street from 12th to Jefferson with arts and entertainment. Features from this earlier festival included a gypsy camp, a miniature Atlantic City, and an entire block transformed into the streets of Cairo. Tens if not hundreds of thousands of people came out for the five-day festival, so many that the newspaper was called to report that "All Virginia is in Richmond."

Festivals come and go. Nothing last forever. June Jubilee began to fizzle in the mid-1990s. I cannot properly mark its end. But what matters most is that it happened at all. After all, every now and again, we need some happy dissidents to shake us from our beaten paths.

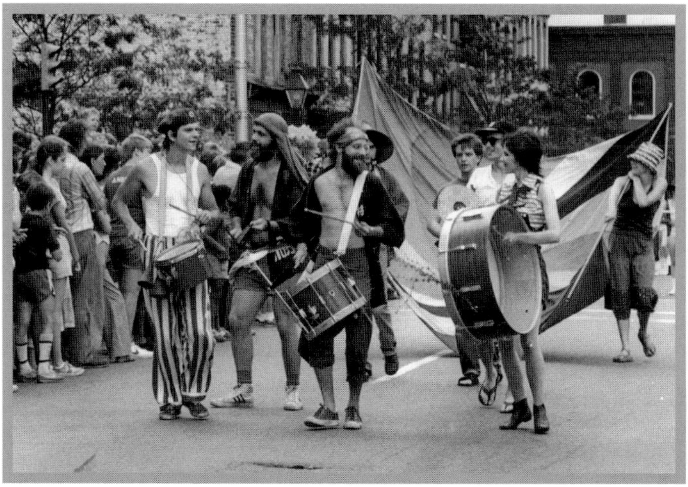

Six Months Orchestra was recognized as the band "Most Likely to Disturb the Peace" at June Jubilee, 1981.

MÉMOIRE

STATUTS ET PROSPECTUS,

CONCERNANT

L'ACADÉMIE

DES SCIENCES ET BEAUX ARTS

DES ÉTATS-UNIS DE L'AMÉRIQUE,

ÉTABLIE A RICHEMOND,

CAPITALE DE LA VIRGINIE;

Par le Chevalier QUESNAY DE BEAUREPAIRE.

A PARIS,

De l'Imprimerie de CAILLEAU, *Imprimeur de l'Académie de* RICHEMOND,

rue Gallande, N°. 64.

1788.

QUESNAY'S ACADEMY

When we are young, our expectations dangle in the air, as if we could be anything at all, king or clown, lion or squirrel. And so too, our fair little City, risen from the James.

In 1776, the Chevalier Quesnay de Beaurepaire set sail for America to join our fight for independence. After distinguished service in our Revolutionary Army, Quesnay floundered through a series of failed ventures in salt and tobacco. But from those early failures, he emerged with a vision to build an academy in the New World as grand as the famous Royal Academy of France. Quesnay's academy would be one of "polite arts" – language, music, painting, sculpture, drama, science, and engineering. And after trial runs in Philadelphia and New York, Quesnay pinned all hope and expectation on Richmond.

Just as Jefferson's Capitol was beginning to rise from Council Chamber Hill, so too was Quesnay's academy, a stone's throw away

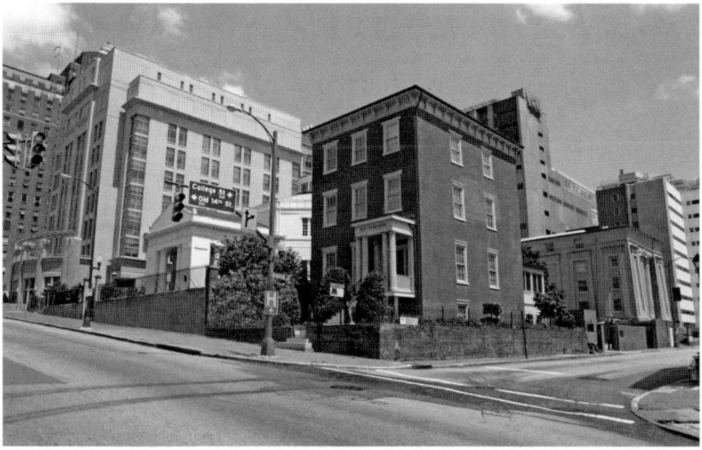

Current site of the block upon which Quesnay's Academy was located.

◄ *Title page of Quesnay's Memoire et Prospectus of the Richmond Academy, 1788.*

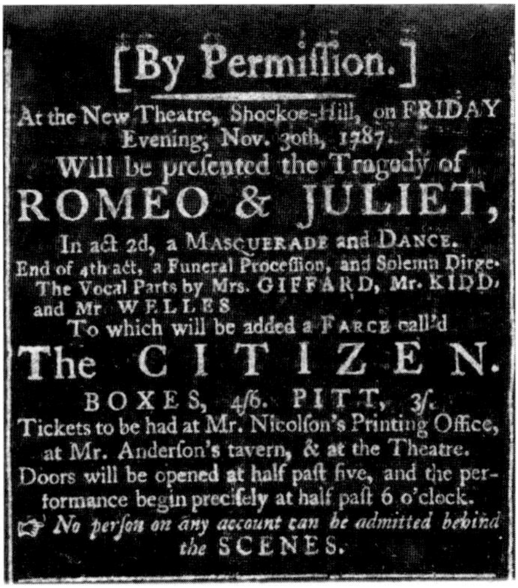

Advertisement typical of the era when Quesnay's Academy was active.

on the square now bounded by 12th, Broad and Marshall. The cornerstones of the academy were set in June 1786 by the venerable Masonic Lodge 13. And in these cornerstones two silver plates were set, one in Latin and the other in French. The plates bore a date inscription that read: "laid … on the festival of St. John the Baptist, in the year of Light, 5786, and of the Vulgar Era, 1786."

Quesnay had supporters far and wide, from the Governor of Virginia to the King of France. Even Benjamin Franklin's daughter sang his praises. But he had detractors too, chief of among them, Thomas Jefferson, then Minister to France. Jefferson cautioned Quesnay against what he called "but a project in the air," doomed by the "poverty, debts, distress and want of money" in our new country.

Quesnay sought to overcome his financial limitations here by an all-out fundraising campaign in Paris. But he was soon sidetracked by the French Revolution and never returned. After his departure, Quesnay's grand academy was used for a theatre – the first regular one in the city. And in 1788, the academy was the only building large enough to house the Virginia Convention as it ratified the federal Constitution. Sadly, the building was gutted by fire in 1798. Just over a decade later, an adjacent theatre also burned down in a tragic fire that inspired our still-standing

The Coat of Arms of Francois Quesnay, grandfather of the founder of the Richmond Academy.

Monumental Church.

From Quesnay's vision, Richmond could have emerged as the arts capital of the New World. And though Jefferson dismissed it as a project in the air, Thoreau would have responded a half century later, "poverty is not poverty, nor weakness weakness. If you have built castles in the air, your work need not be lost; that is where they should be. Now put the foundations under them."

In the 1930s, there was a short-lived effort to revive Quesnay's academy. But this effort ceded to a more compelling need for an art museum. And from that need emerged the Virginia Museum of Fine Arts, perhaps not Quesnay's entire vision, but surely the best of it.

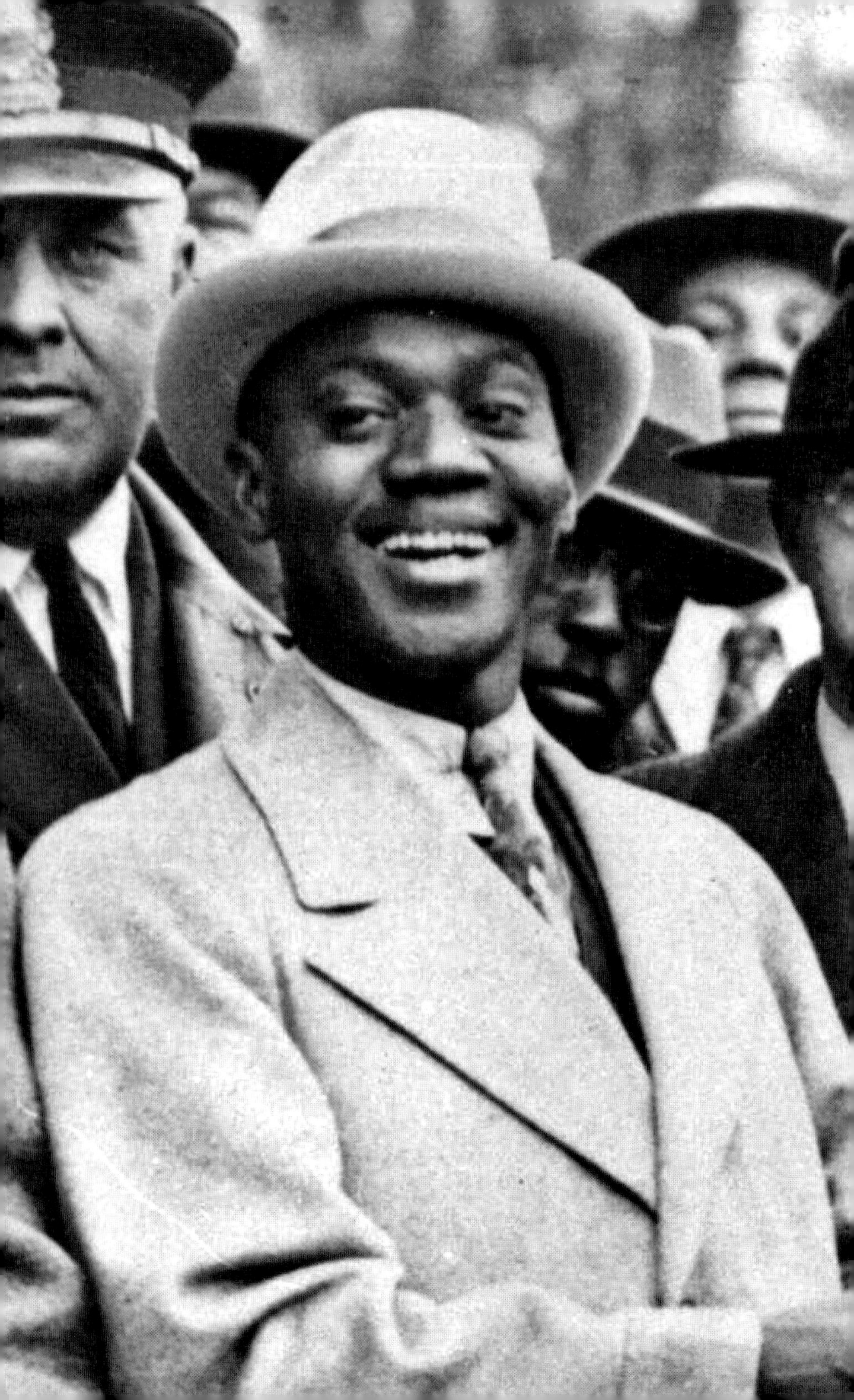

ROBINSON THEATER

It is easy to forget that even the faded scribble scrabble of our sidewalks tell stories. Just consider the one outside of 2903 Q Street up in North Church Hill. Etched into the concrete are the footprints and autograph of Richmond's very own Bill "Bojangles" Robinson, the greatest tap dancer the world has ever known.

Bojangles made these marks in celebration of a new theater named in his honor. The Robinson, as it was known, opened for business on September 29, 1937, amidst thousands of revelers who jammed the streets to witness history in the making. At the event were dignitaries from the City, Virginia Union University, and the National Association of Colored Women. Screen star Fredi Washington appeared in person. Shirley Temple wired her best wishes, and even Bojangles, who had been unexpectedly detained by rehearsals for the Cotton Club Parade, wrote to say that though he was in Hollywood, his heart was in Richmond.

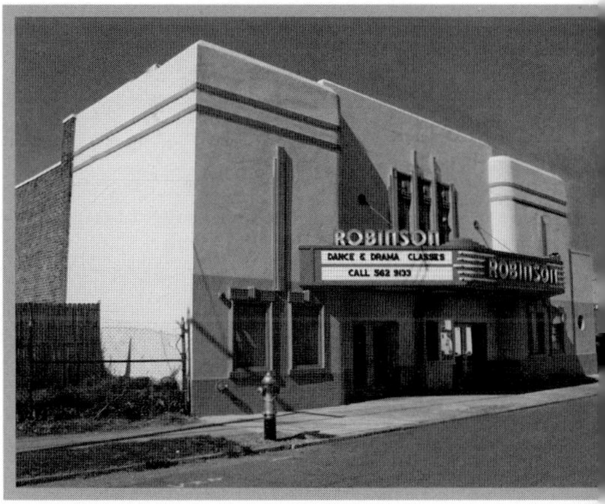

The theater featured "ultra modern" projection and sound equipment and a "dazzling neon marquee." Though it surely had

◄ *Bill "Bojangles" Robinson, Richmond native, actor and dancer, donated the traffic light at Leigh and Adams Streets and Chamberlayne Avenue to protect children crossing the intersection on their way to school. 1933.*

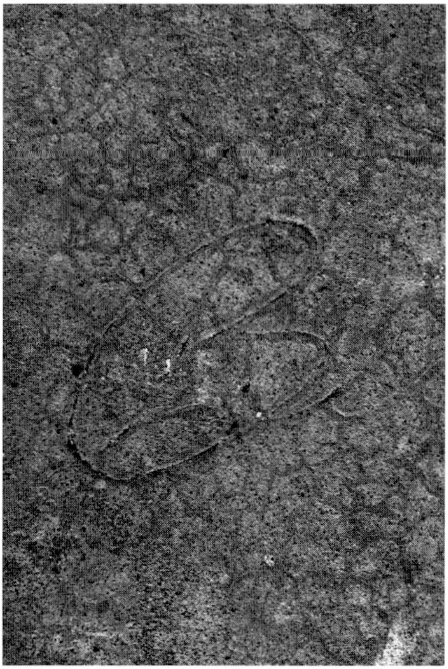

Remains of Bill "Bojangles" Robinson's signature in the concrete in front of the Robinson Theater.

competition in other quarters of the City, the theater was considered to be a landmark in the transformation of North Church Hill. Old-timers still recall with pride the "four corners" on Q, a thriving commercial area for dry goods, clothes, confections, and, of course, movies, music, and other talent at the Robinson. Just around back of the theater, obscured by time and history, is the yard from which car number 28 made the nation's first successful electric trolley trip on January 9, 1888. And across the yard is the old railway depot that for a time was one of Richmond's most revered jazz clubs, rivaling those that lined the Deuce in Jackson Ward.

The Robinson was operated by Abe Lichtman, who also operated the Hippodrome, Globe, Maggie Walker, and Booker T Theaters in Richmond, the Howard and Lincoln Theaters in D.C., and a chain of other so-called "colored" playhouses in the mid-Atlantic. Lichtman also owned the Washington Bears, an all-black basketball team that went 41-0 in 1943 to clinch the World Professional Basketball

Tournament. An incongruous champion of the black community, Lichtman was reportedly held in such esteem that his theaters were untouched during the riots that followed the assassination of Martin Luther King, Jr. in 1968.

Q Street is a different place these days, but its many hints of treasure remain. From behind a construction wall, the Robinson has just recently risen to new life as a community arts center. And with it, perhaps, the soul of the four corners. From the faded scribble scrabble of the sidewalk, I can almost hear the rat-a-tat-tip-tapping of old Bo now.

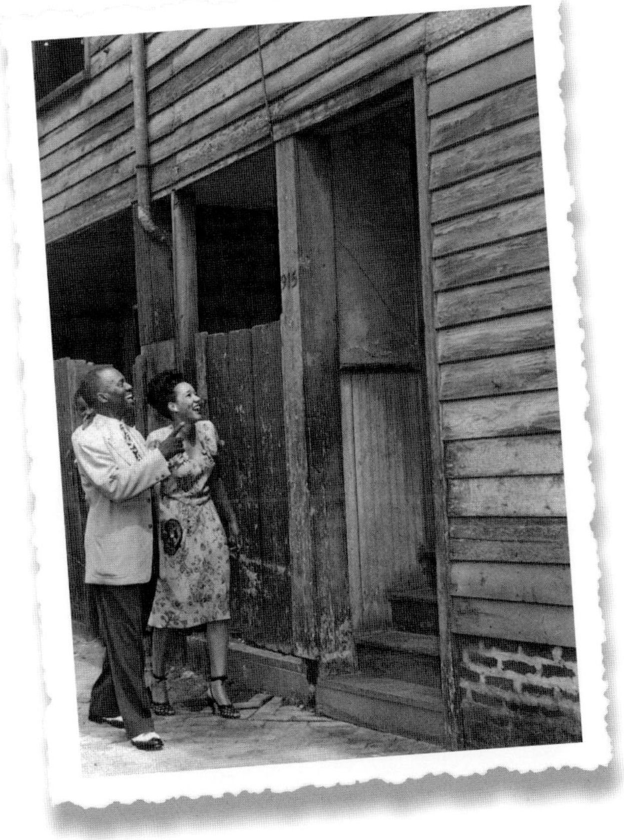

Bill "Bojangles" Robinson and his wife visit the house at 915 North Third Street in Richmond, Virginia, where he was born.

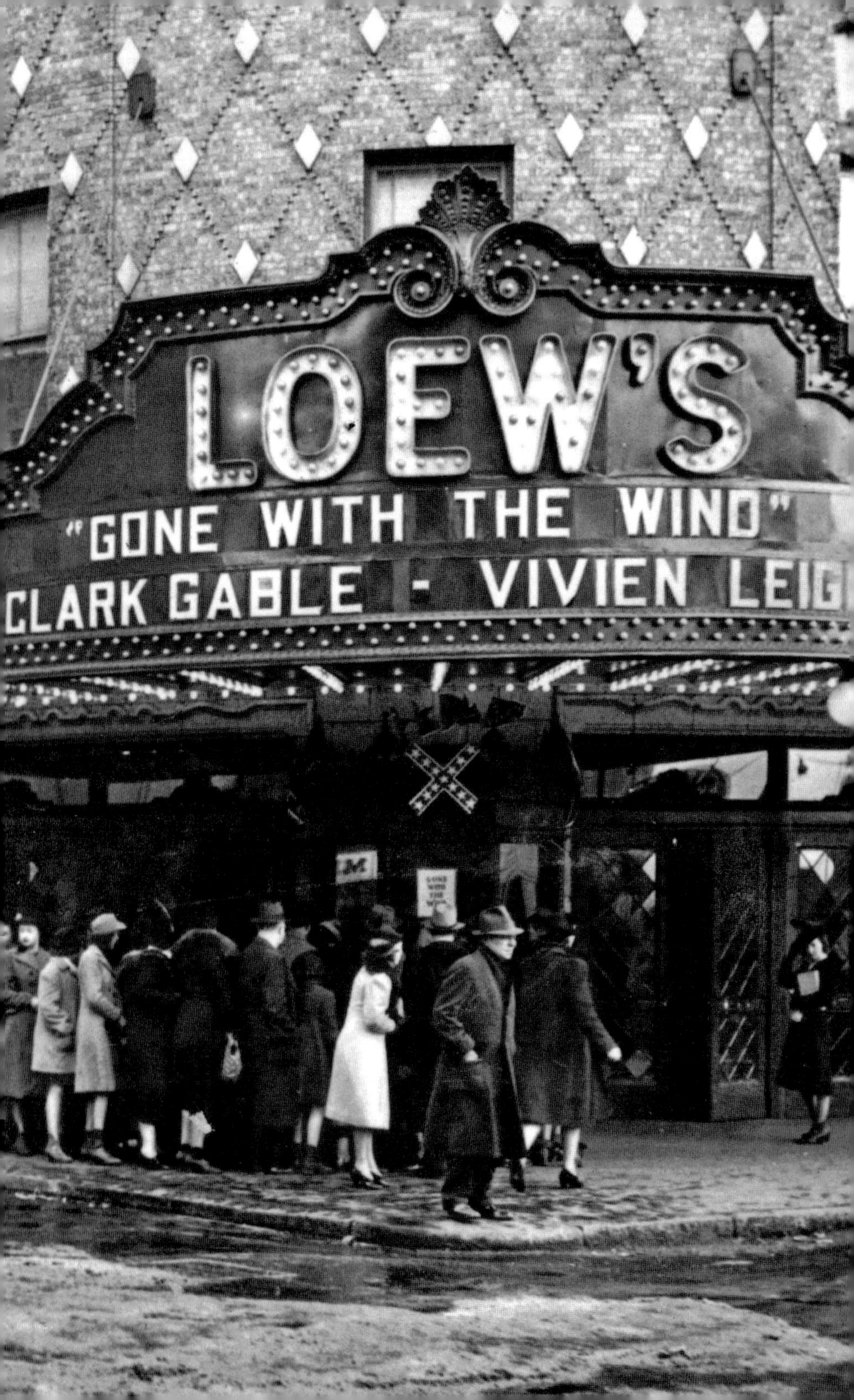
LOEW'S
"GONE WITH THE WIND"
CLARK GABLE - VIVIEN LEIG

Loew's Movie Palace

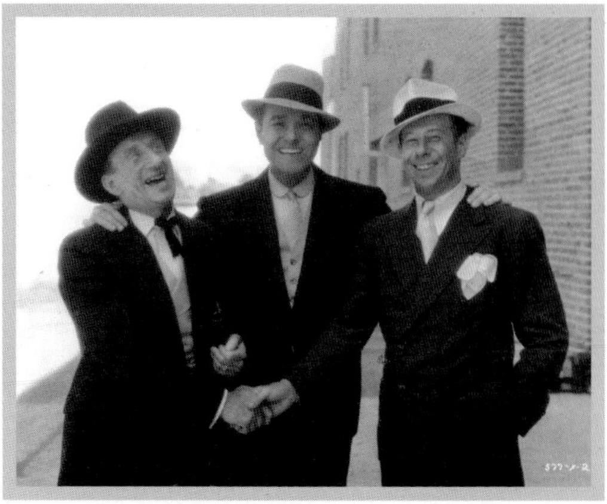

Jimmy Durante (left) and Bert Lahr (right) join in the homecoming visit of native Virginian William Haines, accomplished film actor.

These days, all eyes are on the construction crews bustling around 6th and Grace like so many fugitive carpenter ants. Framed by the glory of hydraulic cranes and technicolor, the scene is not much different than it was back in 1926, when the entertainment mogul, Marcus Loew, first chose this site for Richmond's most spectacular movie palace.

The Loew's Theatre opened its doors to thousands of hopeful fans on April 9, 1928, an otherwise ordinary Monday in our fair City. They came not just for first-run movies from the fabled studios of Metro-Goldwyn-Mayer, but also comedy, news, and other "entertaining novelties." As the announcement read on opening day, "EVERYONE will be there to enjoy the wonders of this unbelievable place – the ten thousand surprises of luxury, color, charm, music, design, courtesy and the whole spirit of the entertainment without rush, hurry or commercial taint."

On opening night, ushers dressed as Bulgarian generals escorted movie-goers to their seats, and a young Texan named Wild Oscar banged out a tympanic rendition of "Hello Richmond" on the Mighty Wurlitzer as his musical greeting to Richmond. Around

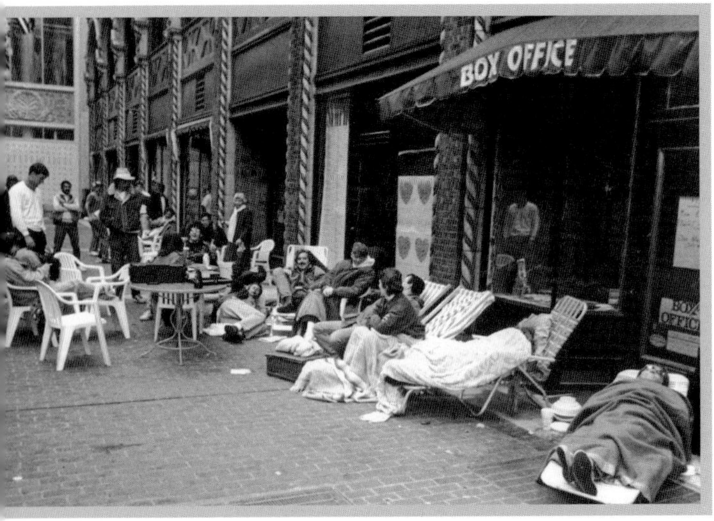

Long lines were seen frequently for events at the Loew's, as shown here in 1990.

this time, Zaban's Box Spring Company on Cary promised to make old mattresses new for the low, low price of six dollars. And the General Electric Company announced a new technology – one born out of fifteen years of top-secret research – a refrigerator that you never had to oil … guaranteed.

The Loew's was tucked between the two most prestigious department stores in the City, along a street once dubbed the "Fifth Avenue of Richmond." From the outside, the theatre looked more like a Spanish mission than a movie house. And from the inside, when the curtain rose and the lights went down, the visual effects conveyed the illusion of being in open air under a starlit sky.

For many years, the theatre would hold contests to locate Richmond's largest movie-going households, and then give them a free Thanksgiving dinner in the lobby as their prize. In the mid-30s, the theatre teamed up with the *News Leader* to bring Hollywood to Richmond to direct and produce an all-talkie motion picture. The movie featured 125 local girls and boys, and premiered before rain-dampened klieg lights at the Loew's on March 27, 1936.

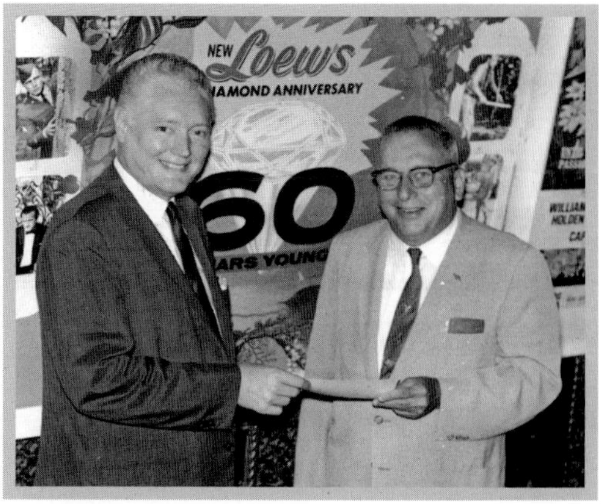

Orville Crouch and George Peters proudly display the National Showmanship Award that was presented to the Loew's in 1964.

Nearly three decades later, the theatre was the scene of nightly protests by students from Virginia Union University – students who wanted nothing more than the right to enjoy the same ten thousand surprises of luxury as their white counterparts. These brave, young leaders picketed the Loew's and the other downtown movie houses until they secured this long denied right in 1963.

Even a starlit sky fades over time. On May 13, 1979, the theatre closed its doors under a marquee that read, "Goodbye Richmond." But of course, every end marks the promise of a new beginning. The theatre soon reopened as a performing arts center, and will reopen yet again amidst much anticipated and well deserved fanfare in the fall of 2009. Ticket prices will surely run higher than the 25¢ morning matinee eight decades ago, but at least this time around, we will *all* get to enjoy it.

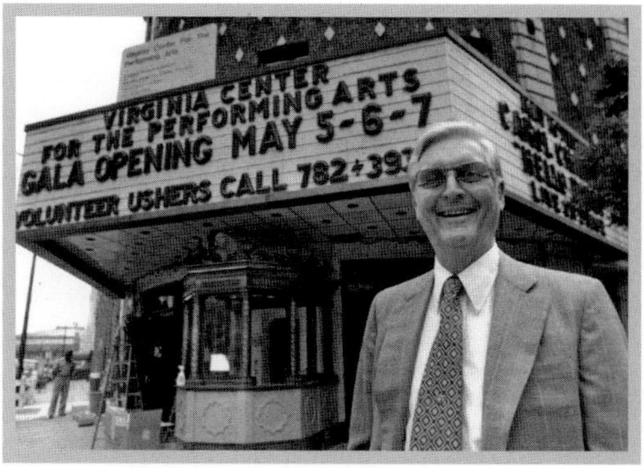

Helmut Wakeham, General Manager of the Virginia Center for the Performing Arts, on Opening Day, 1983.

The Ghost Usher

In Richmond, ghosts, or should I say ghost *stories*, abound. We surely owe these stories to hundreds of years of hard living, to the traumas of conflict and human emotion, and perhaps also, to the quality of light and noise that emanates from the crumbled-down alleyways of our fair City. Whatever their source, we have strange and mysterious tales about brooding nuns, itinerant peddlers, headless brakemen, phantasmal coaches and four, and all manner of other apparitions and spooks, some gay and playful, some grouchy, others simply ethereal.

One of our most famous ghosts is Edgar Allan Poe, or more properly, his disembodied spirit, which is rumored to visit 2315 West Grace, the home of his old friend Susan Talley, and the scene of his last known private reading of *The Raven*. Another is the ghost of Ellen Glasgow, who died while working on a new novel and who returns to 1 West Main in a Sisyphean struggle to complete it.

We have ghostly voices from the tragic theatre fire of 1811 and from the collapse of the Capitol balcony in 1870. At Shirley Plantation, you might hear the creaking floorboards under Aunt Pratt's favorite rocking chair. And a little further downriver, you might see the mannerly old specter that picks only white carnations.

But of all our many ghost stories, my favorite is the one about the ghost usher of the old Loew's Movie Palace, now known as the Carpenter Center and soon to re-open as the jewel of the Richmond CenterStage complex. The story, as told to me by more than one deadly serious eye-witness, involves all of the requisite staging for the spooky and unexplainable: lights that flicker on and off even when they are unplugged; the sounds of singing and dancing even when the building is unattended; and upper-story stained glass windows, inaccessible except by extension ladder, that are routinely found unlatched and open.

But the centerpiece of the story is an usher, dressed in the theatre's opening day, roaring twenties garb of a Bulgarian general with a double-breasted blue coat and brass buttons, who continues to work for no earthly love or money. He is rumored to let visitors into the locked building, to seat guests for the show, and to make his rounds up, down, and even through the stairs of the lobby. As recently as the theatre's groundbreaking celebration in June 2007, our ghost usher was reportedly hard at work, with one volunteer questioning later, "Who's the new guy dressed in the blue coat with brass buttons?"

Not so long ago, some experts in the paranormal spent the night at the old theatre and detected thirteen odd and assorted apparitions. Who knows, instead of one usher, maybe there's an entire corps? Either way, if I were you, I wouldn't talk during the performance.

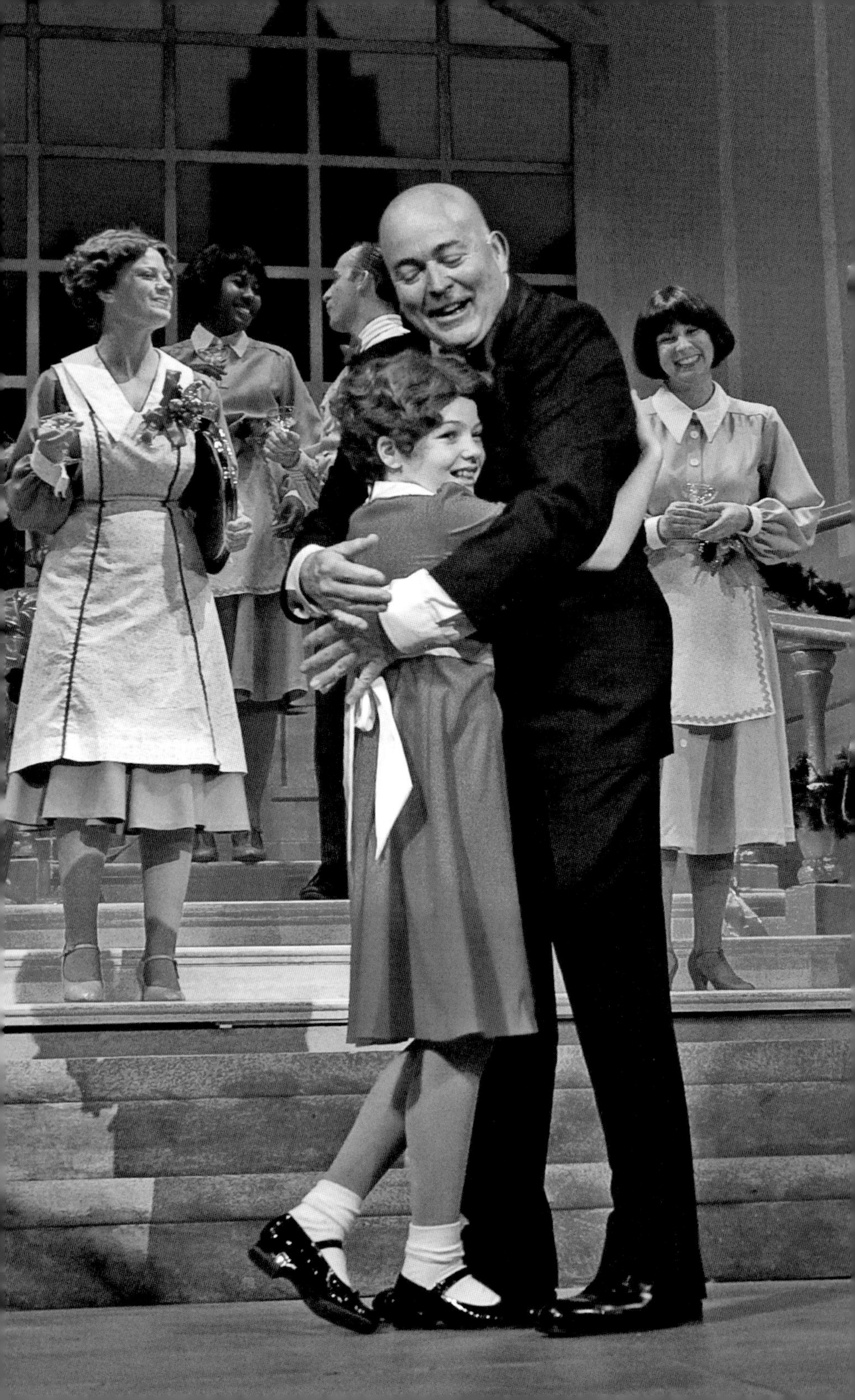

Theatre IV

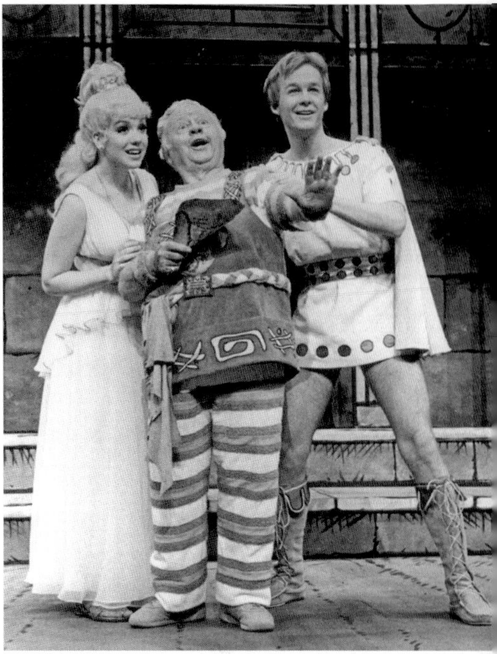

Mickey Rooney is among many recognized actors who have appeared in Theatre IV performances.

In the eyes of a child, nothing is as preposterous as a serious adult. Why, even a 6-foot tall man in a bunny suit, with paws of felt and tail of crushed velvet, is a more credible spokesman for do's and don'ts and that sort of thing. But don't take it from me. Take it from Richmond's most incurably creative men in bunny suits, Phil Whiteway and Bruce Miller.

Thirty-four years ago, Phil and Bruce started the first professional children's theatre in Virginia history, right here in Richmond. And from Halifax High School to Dogwood Dell, from makeshift stages in parks all around our fair City, they parlayed their vision into one of the largest children's touring theatres in the country, one that now serves hundreds of thousands of students in nearly every state in the union.

Their vision, more Utopian than thespian, goes beyond art and education to health and leadership, to impacting whole communities with otherwise inaccessible performance art. In 1983, Phil and Bruce conceived the play, "Hugs and Kisses," using the language of children to

A scene from "Annie."

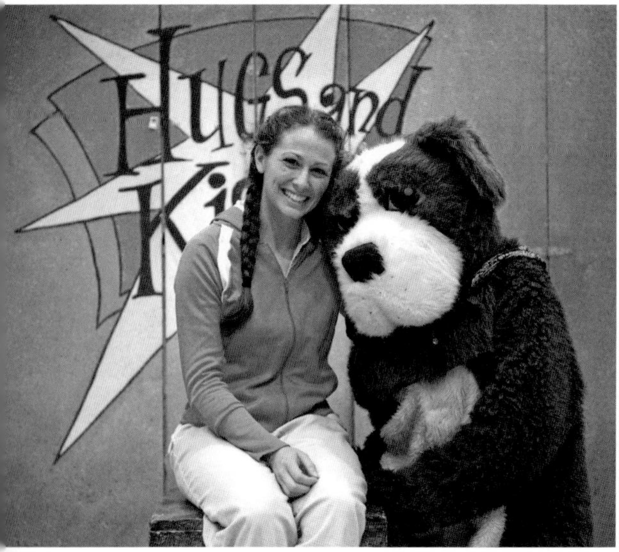

A scene from "Hugs and Kisses."

communicate a theme never before tackled on the professional stage. The play is now the longest running show in Virginia history. It has been performed around the world, and has led to the discovery of over 12,000 cases of child abuse, with hundreds if not thousands of perpetrators behind bars as a consequence.

Many of us know Phil and Bruce from their local anchor at Theatre IV on Broad, and from the larger-than-life, ruby red slippers that deck the marquee whenever they reprise "The Wizard of Oz." But few recall the roots of the space they now inhabit. The old Empire Theatre opened its doors on Christmas Day 1911, closed in 1927, and re-opened as the Booker T in 1934. Next door, the Little Theatre opened in 1912, but closed just four years later due, in no small irony, to its size. After two decades as an outlet store, an auction house, and a Piggly Wiggly, the Little Theatre re-opened as the Maggie Walker in 1936.

In the long, tortured days of segregation, the Booker T and Maggie Walker were among the most prominent of Richmond's colored theatres. And their importance to the continued healing of our now united City is not lost on either Phil or Bruce, who believe that the roots of their Theatre IV space are vital to accessing and engaging our entire community. Among many distinctions, Theatre IV is the single largest producer of African American history programs in the United States.

So, if you happen to see two men in bunny suits hopping down Broad or tackling some other theatrical delight, remember that their path is a singular one, from darkened stage to white hot light, and our collective path is better for it. Phil and Bruce, this encore is for you.

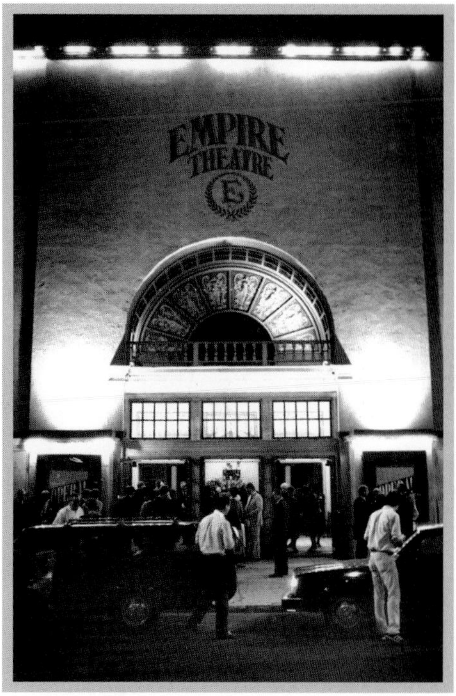

The Empire Theater occupied this building from 1911 to 1927.

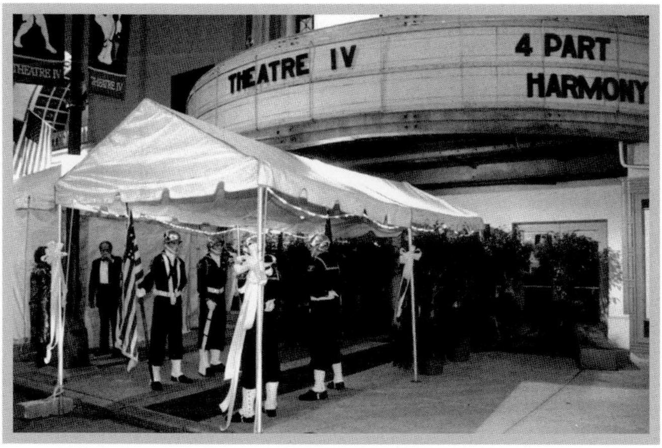

Opening gala for the performance, Four Part Harmony.

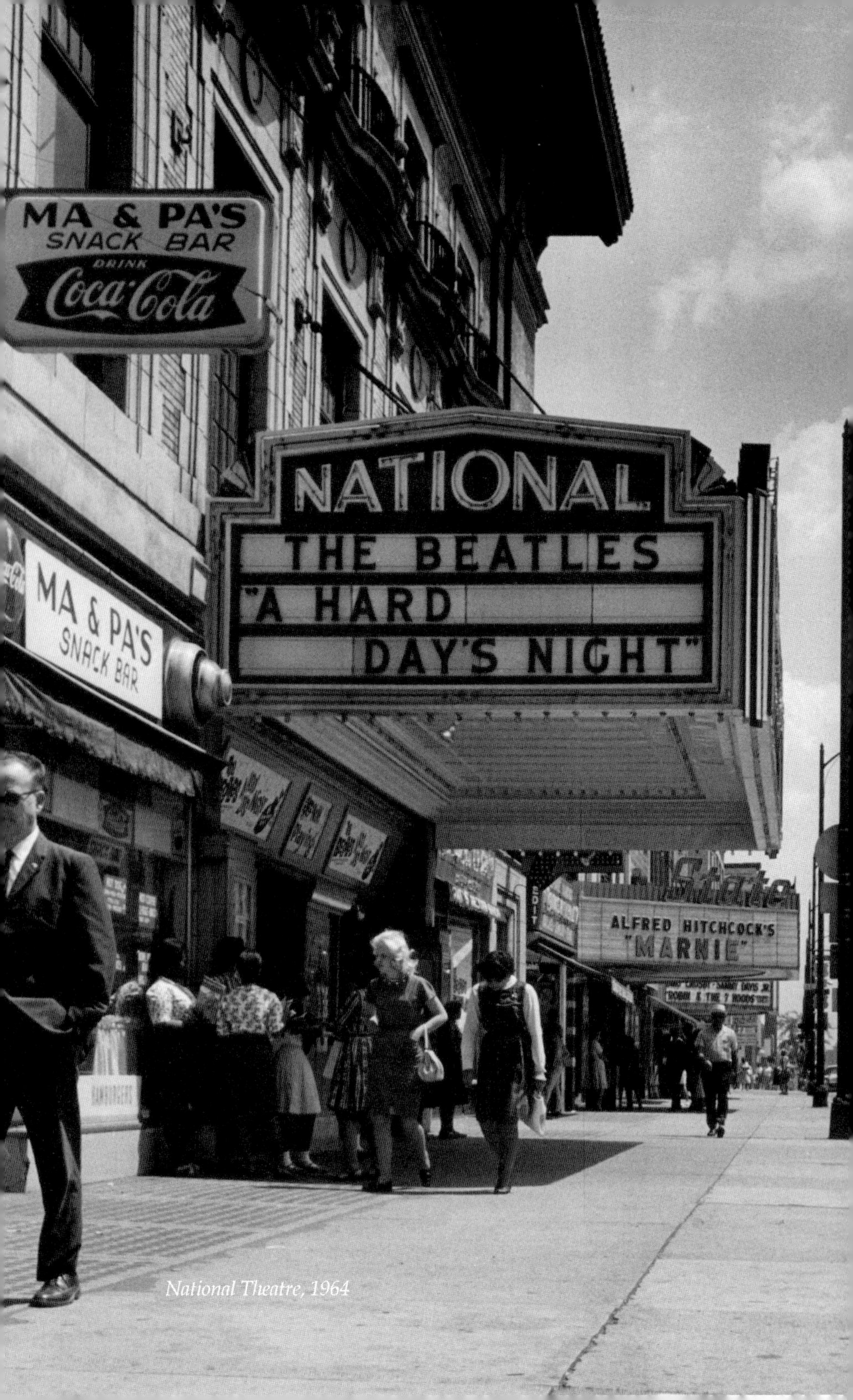

National Theatre, 1964

THE NATIONAL

The National is the hottest card in town. With ambience, edge, and rocking good music, it is no surprise that lines are beginning to form again down on Broad Street, something that has not happened in a long, long time. And what's good for the audience is even better for the bands. During their gigs, performers get to enjoy a floating stage. And afterwards, well, if they want, they can float awhile in the oversized, backstage hot tub. How's that for star treatment?

The National is more than a preeminent stage in our fair City. It is a preeminent stage *with pedigree*.

The National Theatre opened on November 11, 1923, with newspaper headlines proclaiming that it was the "most strikingly lovely playhouse in the South." Among its many distinctions were chairs with "automatic spring-edge hydraulic cushions;" the

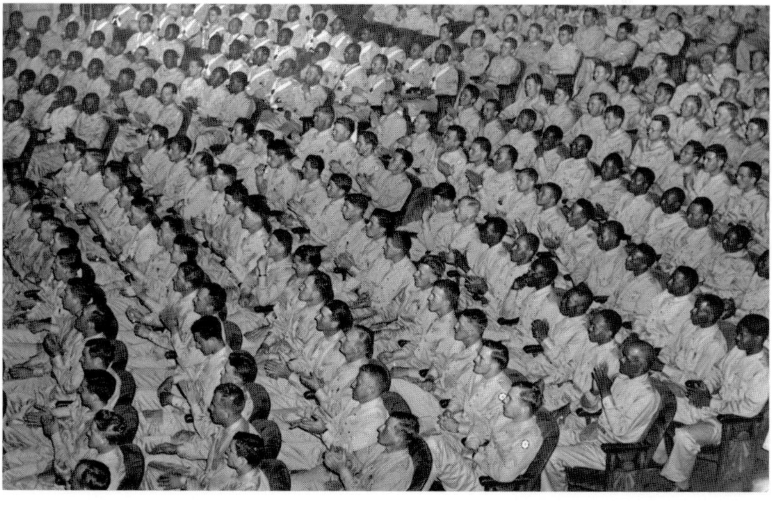

The National Theatre was the scene of a World War II All Soldiers Audience Event. 1943.

largest orchestra pit in Virginia; free afternoon tea in the ladies' room; Haskins Billiard Academy, the City's largest pool hall, in the basement; and Tip Toe Inn, an attached restaurant that featured pastries, candies, ices, and the "only mechanically refrigerated soda fountain" this side of the Mississippi.

Despite the Depression and Prohibition, there was a promising mood in Richmond. And for a mere ten cents, with war tax included, children could wile away the afternoon with Burt Hollowell conducting the National Theatre's Symphony Orchestra and Robert Rodwell at the helm of the Mighty Voiced Organ.

The National Theatre featured movies, vaudeville, and even burlesque shows like the "Girlie-Go-Round Revue." It also boasted the best Broadway-style stage in the City. In April 1934, Katherine Cornell stole the house with the

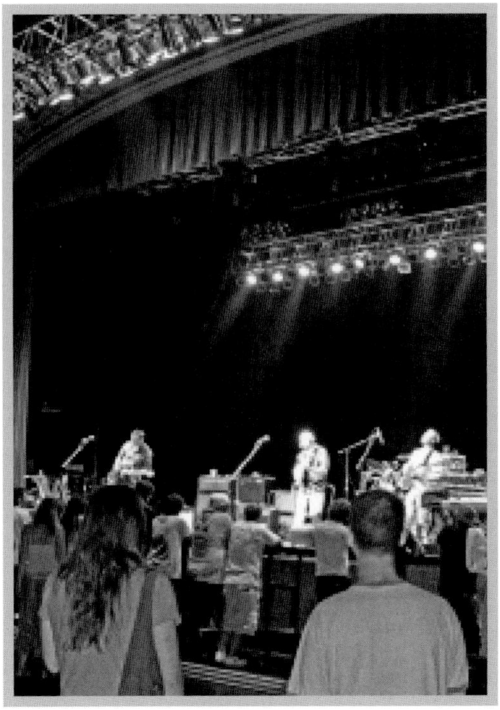

The Richmond band, 11th House, at The National, August 1, 2009.

comedy, "The Barretts of Wimpole Street," featuring the late-great Orson Welles as Octavius Moulton-Barrett and Basil Rathbone as Robert Browning.

Alas, nothing and no one are safe from the irreducible realities of evolution. In 1968, the National Theatre was stripped of its marquee and renamed the Towne Theatre Movie Emporium. The Towne outlasted every other movie house in the City, but eventually succumbed to the suburban movieplexes in 1983. The grand old theatre building almost met with the wrecking ball a year later, but was reprieved in the nick of time by local preservationists. For the next two decades, the building idled unused through a series of redevelopment plans, all of which failed, for better or worse.

And then, like the Phoenix, the National rose again. It now represents the best of the new energy that has infiltrated the downtown arts and cultural district. Despite the Recession and a middling overdose of Consumption, there remains a promising mood in Richmond. This time around, though, let's not forget that it is a mood *with pedigree*.

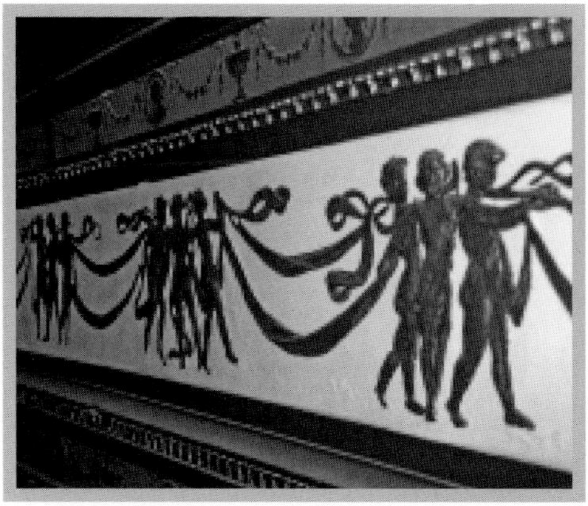

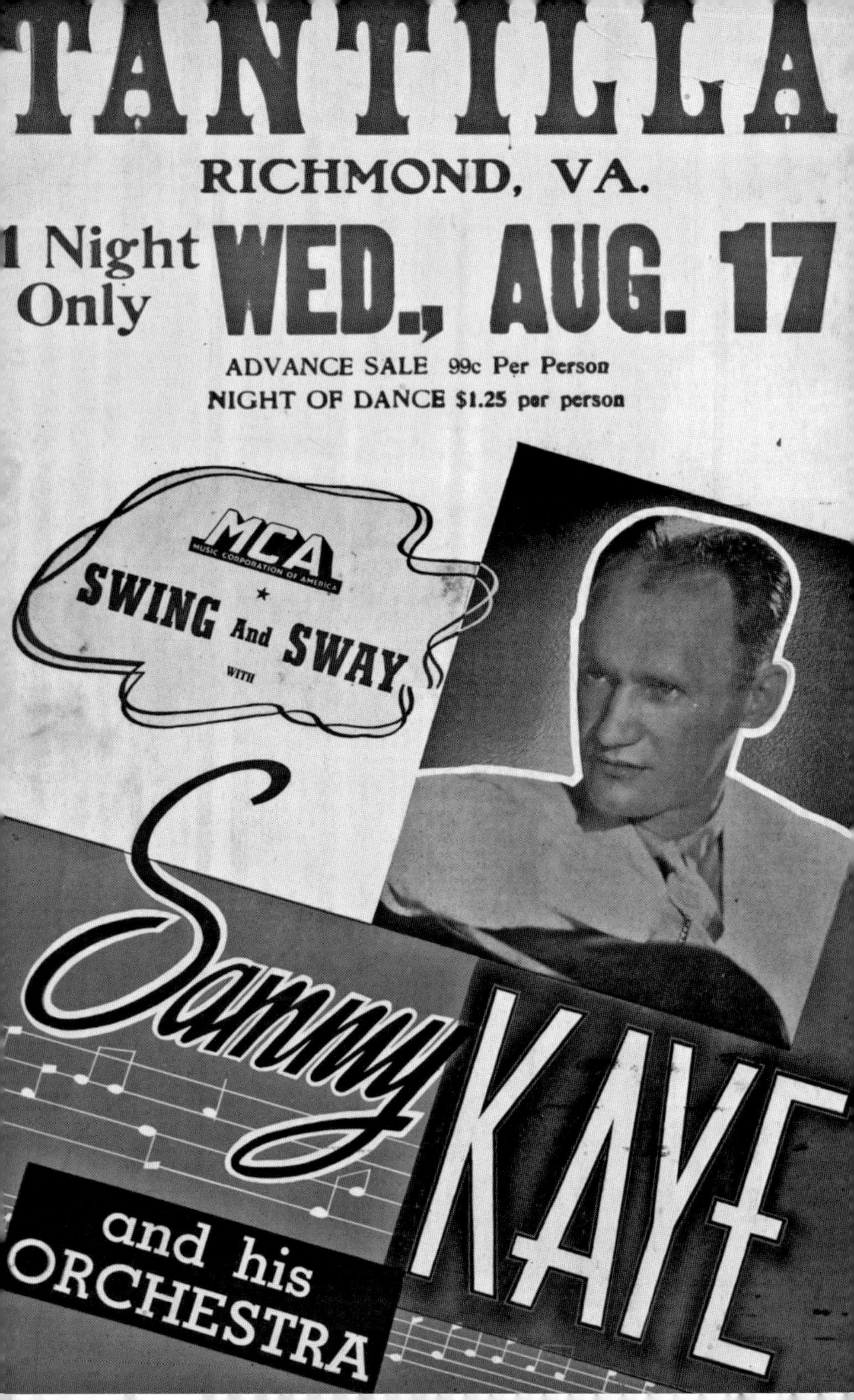
TANTILLA
RICHMOND, VA.
1 Night Only
WED., AUG. 17
ADVANCE SALE 99c Per Person
NIGHT OF DANCE $1.25 per person
MCA
MUSIC CORPORATION OF AMERICA
SWING And SWAY
WITH
Sammy
KAYE
and his ORCHESTRA

Tantilla Garden

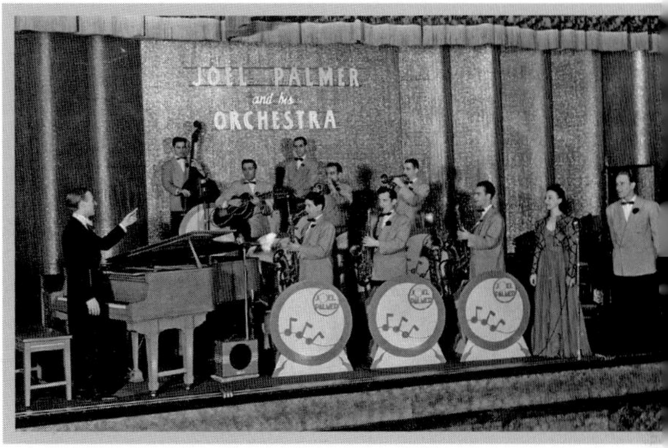

The Joel Palmer Orchestra.

On June 15, 1933, amidst headlines that proclaimed the darkening clouds of unrest in Europe, a little patch of paradise opened on Broad. It was a place for dancing and romancing, and throughout its legendary 36 year run, it was known as Tantilla Garden.

Tantilla was the kind of place where decorous lovers went to court and "brown-bag" their cocktails from darkened corners of the ballroom; where long-married couples smiled and nodded away the hours in seats reserved just for them; and where weary servicemen would come to forget about the worries of war or the want of peace. It was also the kind of place where everyone stood a chance of preserving a memory with a matchbook autographed by a jazz headliner like Duke Ellington, Tommy Dorsey, Stan Kenton, or Benny Goodman.

But these visiting greats were not always the main attraction. For many years, Tantilla's house band was led by Babe Barnes, who closed every night with the sentimental favorite, "Good Night, Sweetheart." The legendary big band leader, Bill Zickafoose, also played Tantilla after taking over for Glenn Miller in Europe during World War II. Even Pleasants "Snowball" Crump, the world-renowned tap dancer, was a regular. When he clogged, bucked, and winged, people would make pious offerings of coins onto the stage, so many that Snowball would

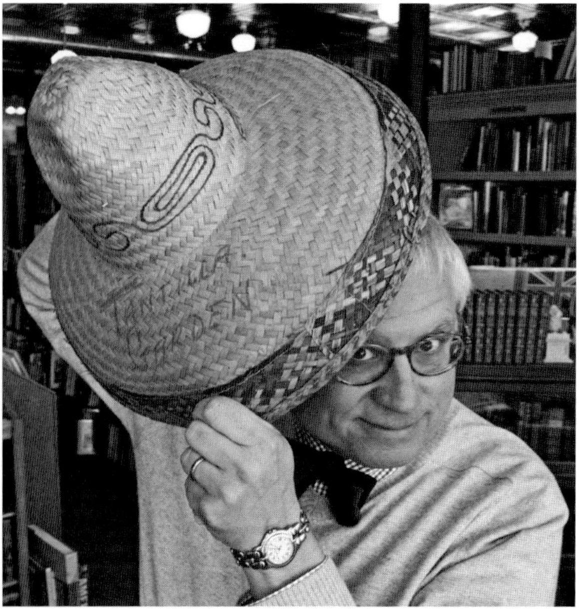

Nick Cook, owner of Black Swan Books, reminisces about Tantilla by showing off a straw hat from an event there.

use brooms to sweep them all up.

Sometimes, paradise emerges by accident, and that is surely the case for Tantilla Garden. The building that housed the dance hall was originally designed for an indoor golfing range. After a few years, this design ceded to a 27-lane bowling alley known as Tiny Town. Only later did the owners conceive and build Tantilla upstairs. Perhaps as an apology for the noisy lanes down below, they also added a retractable roof that offered revelers a chance to dance under the stars.

On March 22, 1969, amidst headlines that proclaimed the darkening clouds of unrest in the jungles of Vietnam, nearly 1,300 people crowded into Tantilla to celebrate and mourn, in equal parts, its last big show. Among them was manager "Red" Wyatt, who had been there since opening day 36 years earlier. Babe Barnes closed the show with a twist, playing "Auld Lang Syne" instead of "Good Night, Sweetheart." And even Snowball Crump made a surprise appearance around midnight, emerging through the backdoor as he had done so many times before.

After the final curtain call, Tantilla Garden was razed for a parking

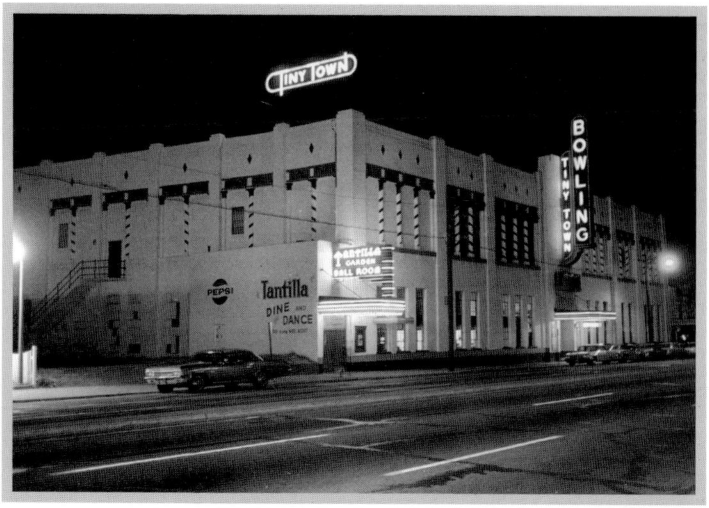

lot. But even then, nostalgia for that little patch of paradise ran high. Demolition bricks ran 25 cents apiece, and to this day throughout our fair City, people covet bits and pieces of Tantilla.

In 1980, Tantilla Garden was revived as the theme of the National Tobacco Festival Queen's Ball at the Holiday Inn. But like Shel Silverstein's woodpecker pecking at a plastic tree, things just weren't as sweet as they used to be.

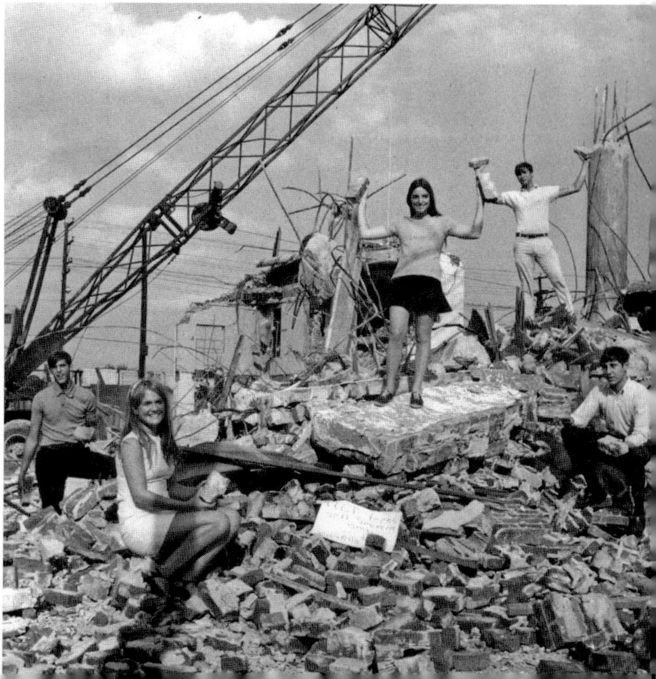

The United Way initiated a fundraising project involving the sale of the bricks following the demolition of Tantilla, 1969.

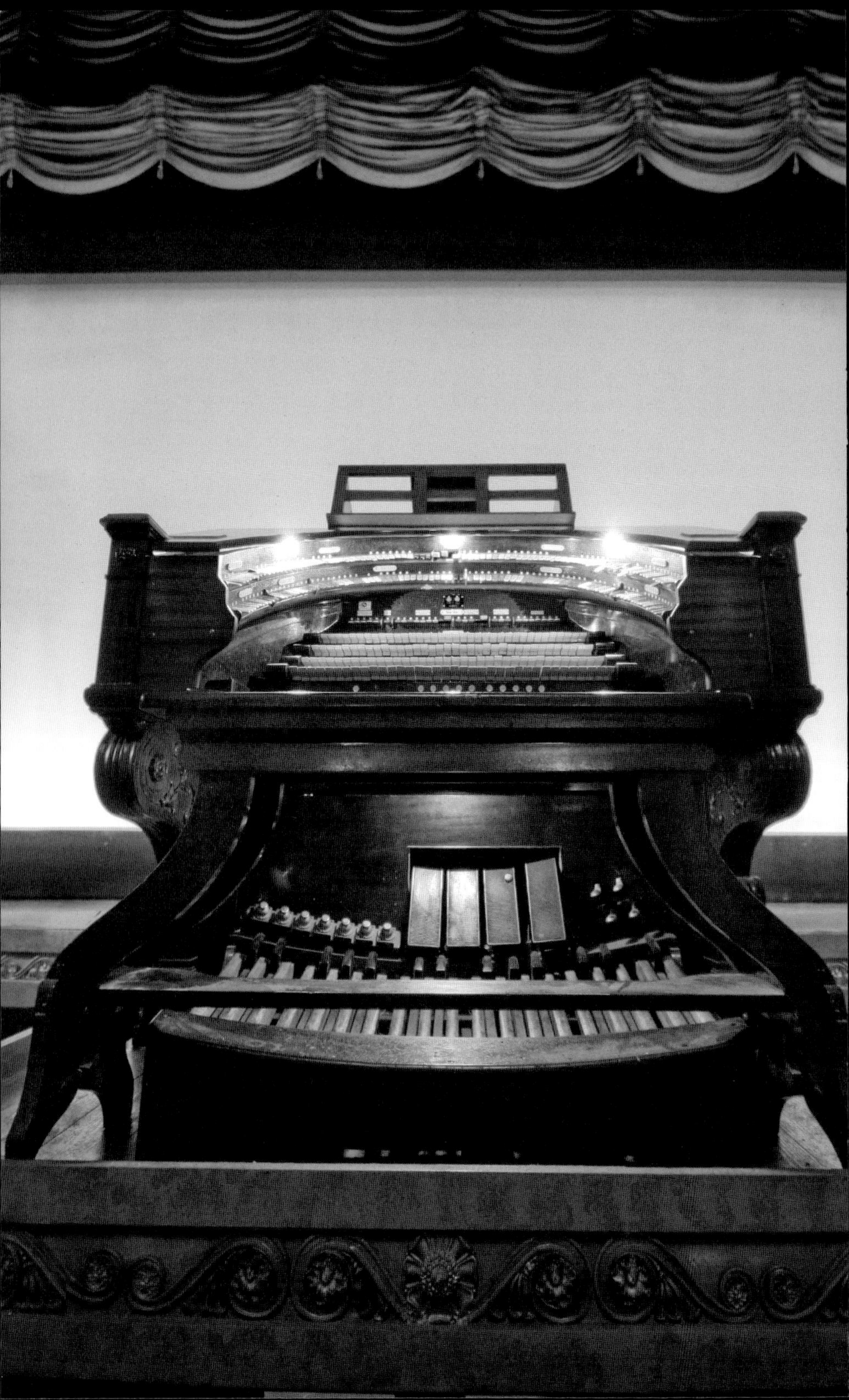

The Byrd and Her Mighty Wurlitzer

When I was little in the way of a child, and the whole world teetered on each new discovery, my brother and I spent many long hours drawn over the battle lines of Risk and other games of destiny. And in the tempest of battle, in the moment of triumph or despair, we would blast Tchaikovsky's *1812 Overture* like mad organists tramping the bellows, and our house would quake at the mighty noise.

I know of only one place in Richmond that captures the flights and fancies of childhood, the illusion of majesty, the dim roar of destiny. It is just up the street in Carytown, a palace unlike any other. The Byrd Theatre opened on Christmas Eve 1928, its velvet drapes and mohair seats the parables of luxury. The Byrd boasts eleven Czechoslovakian crystal chandeliers, the largest laden with 500 lights and 5,000 crystals. But the theatre's rapture is its noise.

The Byrd is home to a theatre pipe organ, a Mighty Wurlitzer, with four manuals and seventeen ranks, with the sounds of tuba, mandolin, marimba, English horn, glockenspiel, clarion, and kettle drum. The console has special effect toggles for whistling wind,

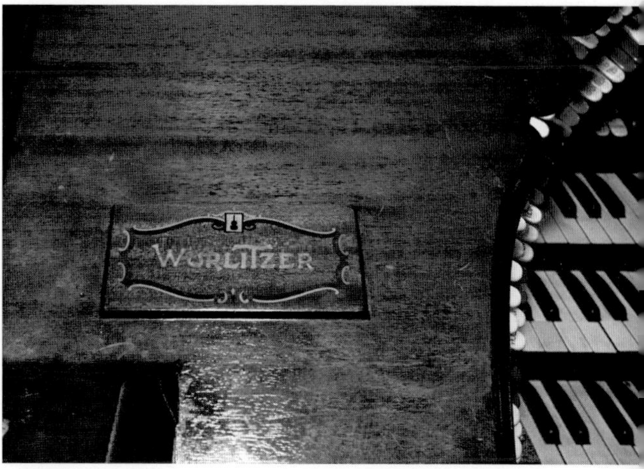

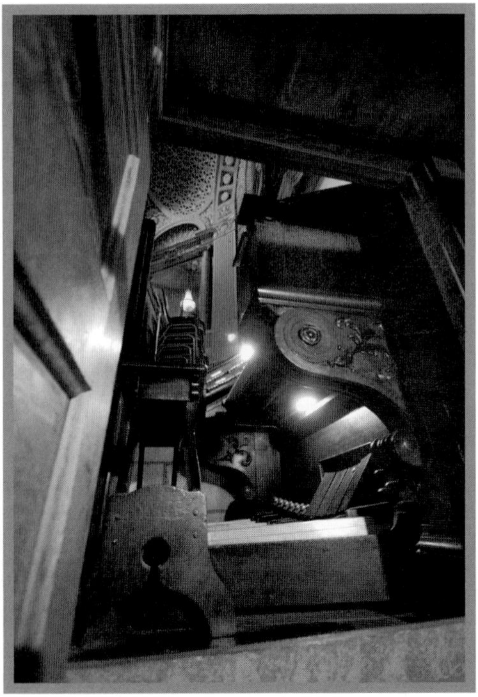

rolling surf, fire gong, horse hoof, and something not unlike the purr of Fidel Castro's cat. But the console is just the wizard behind the curtain. The organ itself is located in hidden rooms on the fourth floor, rooms crammed high with pipes, drums, bells, and horns – the effects all real, their sound forced through a chute like elephants in the basement and trumpeter swans in the belfry, their volume checked and channeled by louvered walls.

There are only a handful of theatre pipe organs left in all of Virginia, and our fair City boasts at least three of them. There are only eleven original movie palaces, most of them shuttered or retooled for more austere entertainment. But the Byrd still offers a nightly movie roll, and on Saturday

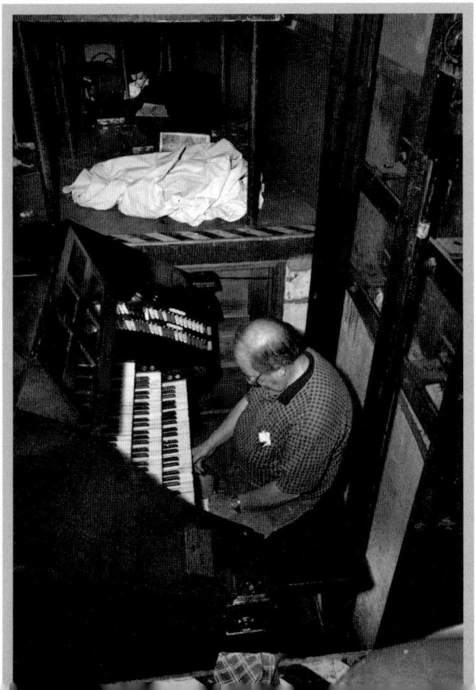

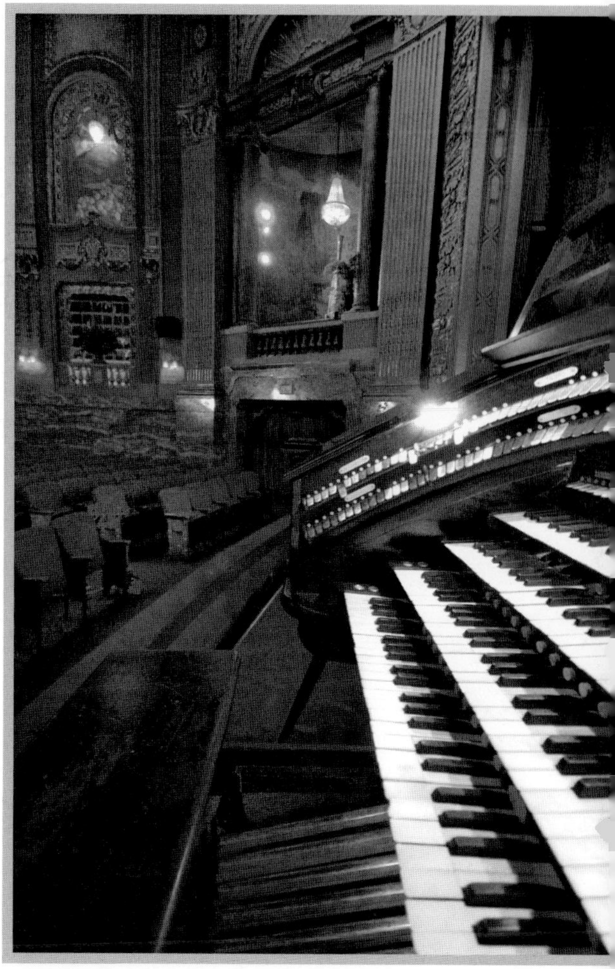

night, the Mighty Wurlitzer still ascends from the console pit to delight the ever-inspired throngs.

The Byrd is our Radio City Music Hall, our Fox Theatre, our Palace Showplace. And under the chink of Czechoslovakian crystal, the opening tremolo of the Mighty Wurlitzer can transport an entire audience to the mysteries of childhood or the Grand Canyon at sundown.

Play on, oh magic, tramping piper. And lead us rumbling into rapture.

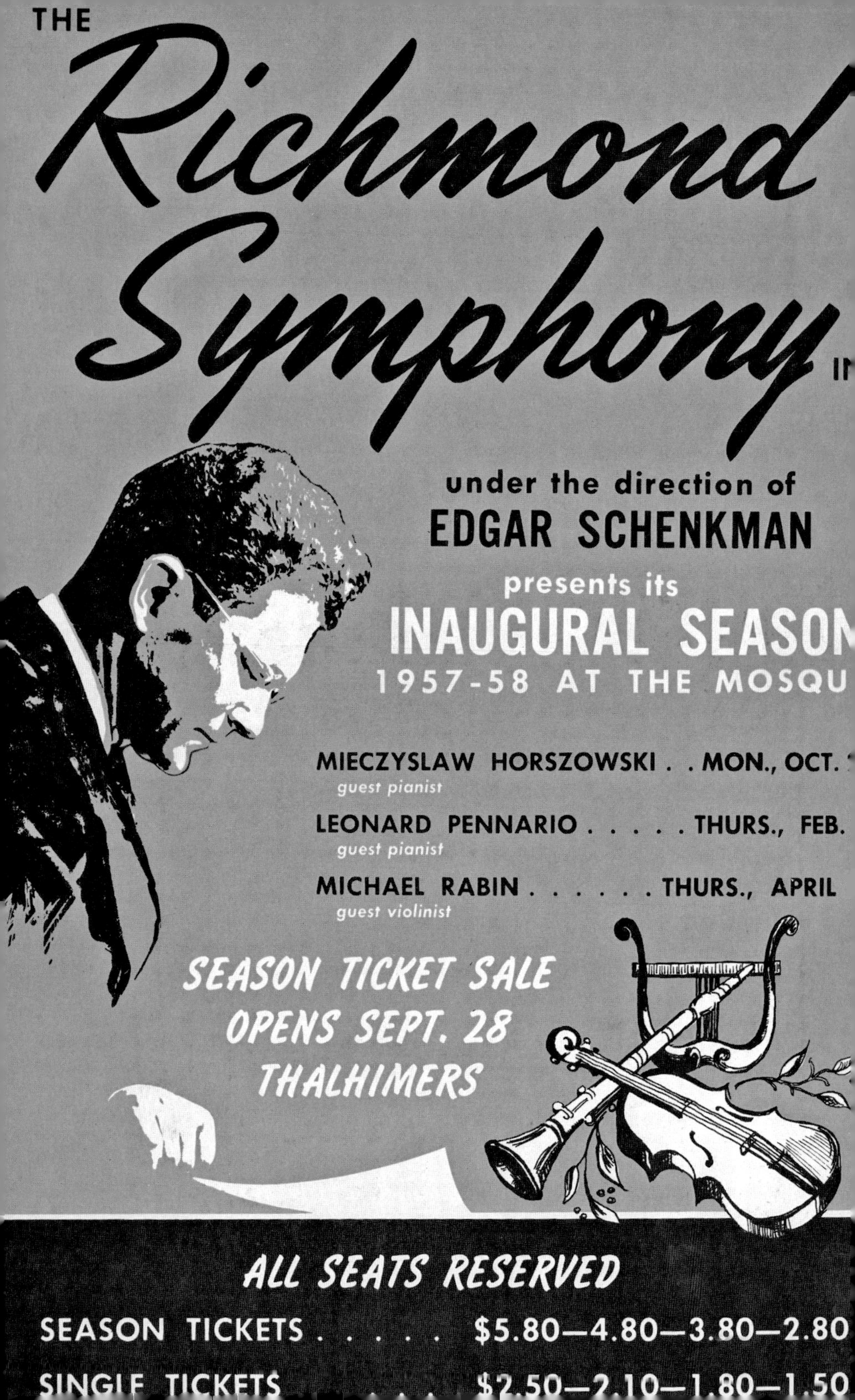
THE
Richmond Symphony
under the direction of
EDGAR SCHENKMAN
presents its
INAUGURAL SEASON
1957-58 AT THE MOSQU
MIECZYSLAW HORSZOWSKI . . MON., OCT.
guest pianist
LEONARD PENNARIO . . . . . THURS., FEB.
guest pianist
MICHAEL RABIN . . . . . . THURS., APRIL
guest violinist
SEASON TICKET SALE
OPENS SEPT. 28
THALHIMERS
ALL SEATS RESERVED
SEASON TICKETS . . . . . $5.80—4.80—3.80—2.80
SINGLE TICKETS $2.50—2.10—1.80—1.50

SYMPHONY

Radio Hall of Famer Karl Haas hosted the longest running classical music program in American broadcasting history. His *Adventures in Good Music* was a window into both the favorite and the forgotten, and his themes were always as affable as his "Hello Everyone!" greeting. In spite of gloomy predictions, Maestro Haas refused to believe that the days of classical music would ever end. Lucky for us, he was right.

Richmond boasts a rich classical music heritage, anchored by a symphony that for over fifty years has brought its joyful noise into performance halls, parks, and classrooms throughout our fair City and beyond. This fall, the symphony will enjoy a homecoming of sorts, returning to the Carpenter Center for a new season that will feature both a new music director and a something-for-everyone repertoire, from Beethoven's *Emperor* to Prokofiev's *Peter and the Wolf*, from Saint-Saens to Simply Sinatra.

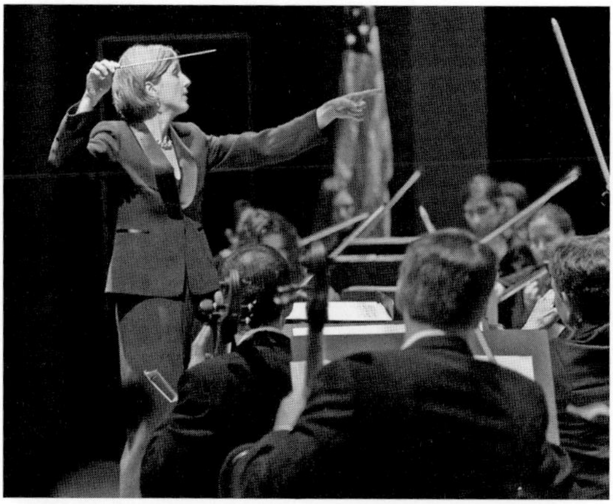

Associate Conductor Erin R. Freeman in rehearsal at The Steward School, September, 2008.

But in this measure of silence before the curtain rises, pray remember the remarkable journey of our homegrown symphony, from a fledgling orchestra struggling to be heard to one of the

Original Richmond Symphony Poster, 1957.

finest metropolitan orchestras in the country. Since the symphony's sell-out debut at the Mosque on October 28, 1957, it has given us musical treats of every flavor. In 1968, Aaron Copeland conducted his scores of *Billy the Kid* and *Appalachian Spring*. In 1976, the one-and-only Karl Haas conducted the symphony's chamber music ensemble. And a year later, the symphony initiated an American Pops series headlined by Sarah Vaughan, Charlie Byrd, and Benny Goodman. Around this same time, the symphony broadened its base to children with a lollipop concert hosted by the beloved Sesame Street performer, Bob McGrath.

Pick any year over its half-century run and the symphony surely left some musical imprint on our City. But its legacy is not music alone. In the early 1960s, Thomas Bridge and Joe Kennedy, Jr. became the first African American musicians to perform with the symphony. And in 1971, Dr. Bridge became the first African American to conduct it.

The year 1957 may seem like along time ago, but the City's symphonic roots actually date back twenty-five years earlier to 1932, when a Californian named Wheeler Beckett chose Richmond over Atlanta to organize the first professional symphony in the South. On May 24, 1932, Maestro Beckett called a meeting at the Hotel John Marshall to share his improbable plan. By June, he had attracted over one

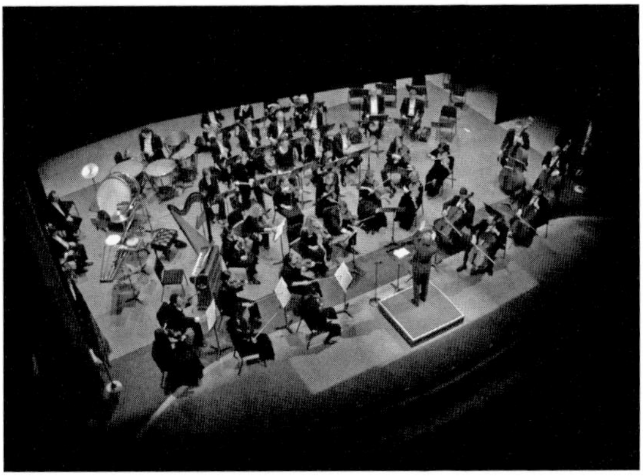

Richmond Symphony rehearsal, Steward School, September, 2008.

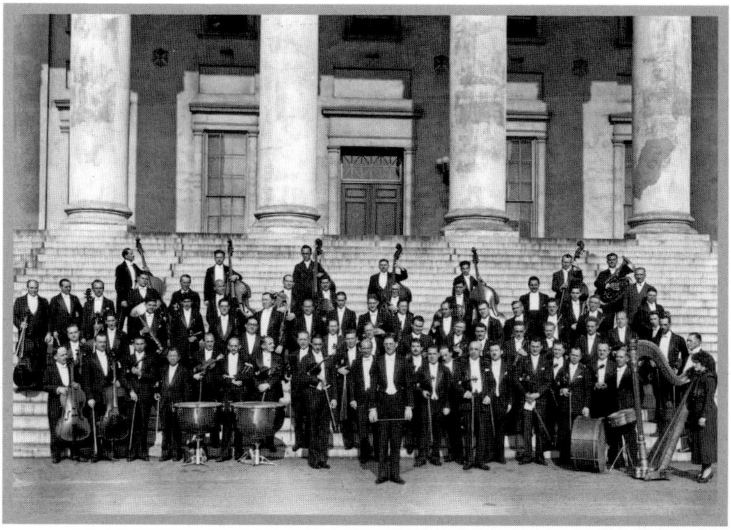

Richmond Symphony Orchestra, 1933.

hundred founding members. And by October, he had blown through nearly every recital hall in New York City auditioning and recruiting professional musicians to join him in Richmond. Maestro Beckett's symphony debuted before a sell-out crowd at the Mosque on November 28, 1932, with as much fanfare from the press as the horn section.

Alas, this first symphony did not survive more than a few years, and it is nearly forgotten today. But even then, some Richmonders must have had in mind a second coming, refusing to believe that the days of classical music would ever end. Lucky for us, they were right.

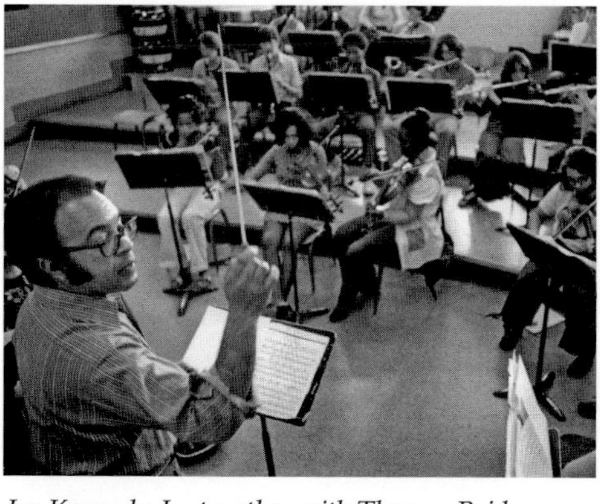

Joe Kennedy, Jr., together with Thomas Bridge, became the first African American musicians to perform with the Richmond Symphony, 1960s.

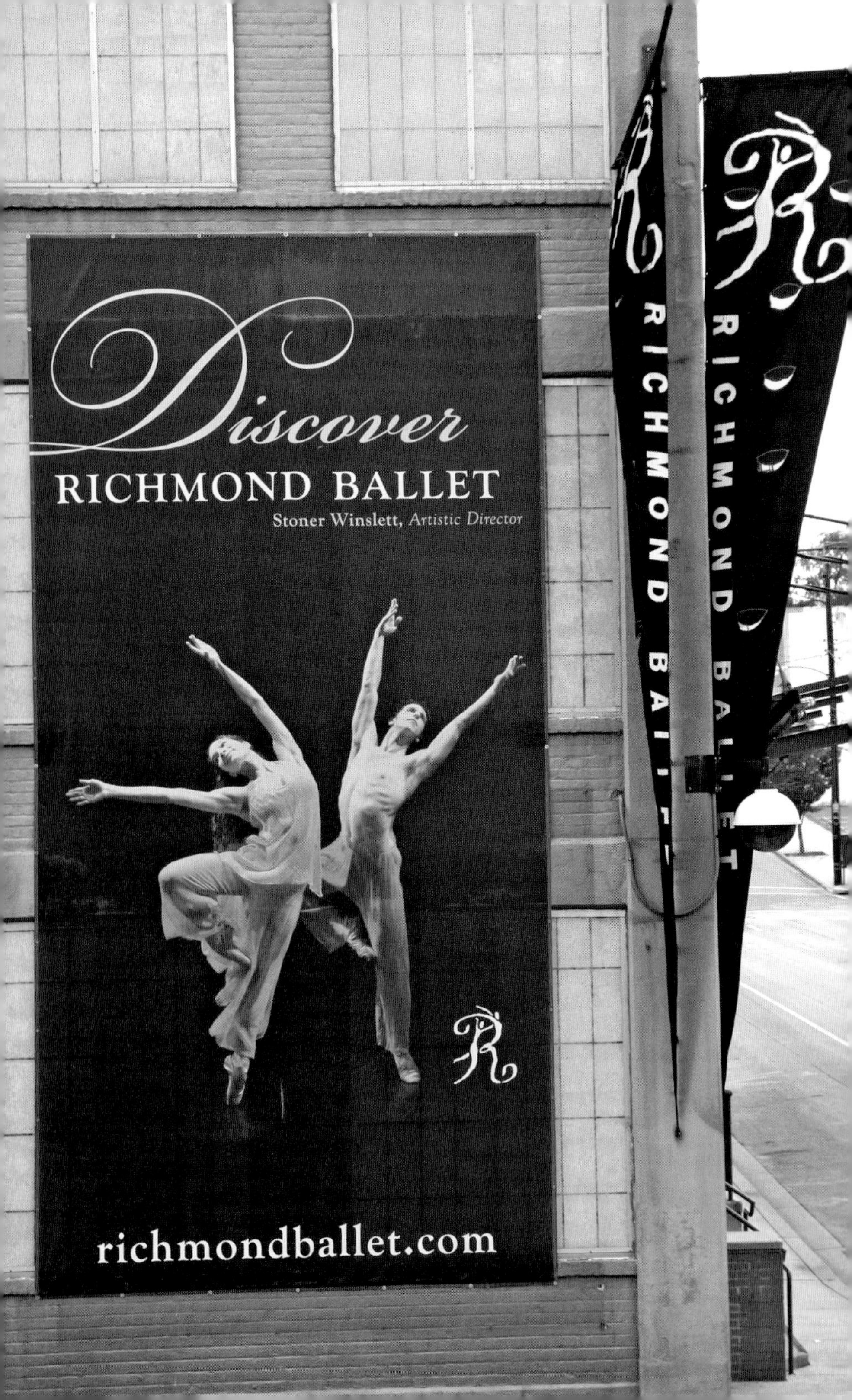
Discover
RICHMOND BALLET
Stoner Winslett, Artistic Director
richmondballet.com
RICHMOND BALLET
RICHMOND BALLET

Ballet

Unlike a piece of art, ballet only lives by performance. It is passed down as oral history, and through its retelling, is made real.

In Richmond, we owe a debt of gratitude to the "board ladies" who helped to establish our ballet in the 1950s, some of whom continue to serve today, over a half century later. In the early days, our ballet was just an amateur troupe comprised mostly of local high school students. Today, the Richmond Ballet is fully professional. It stole New York City in its debut appearance in 2005, and in April 2010, will complete its fourth Big Apple tour in five years.

Richmond Ballet's success is not accidental. The first transformative moment came in 1975, when its organizers founded the School of Richmond Ballet. The second came in 1980, when they

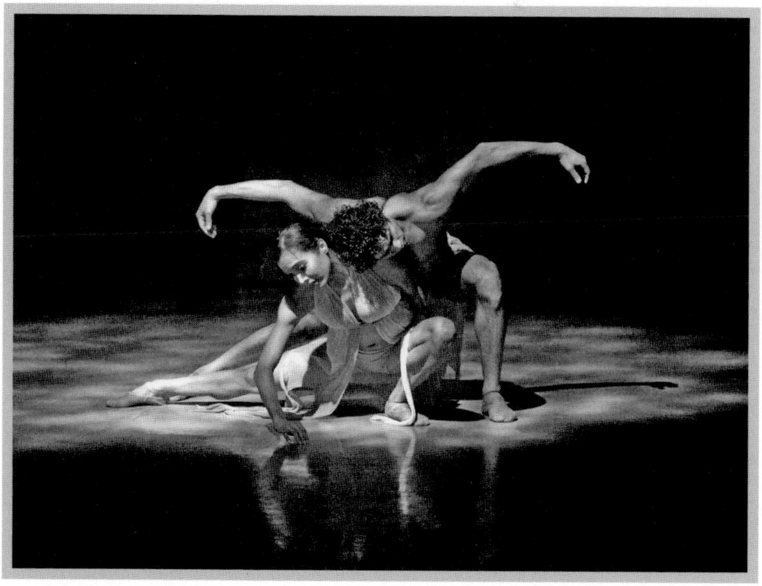

Maggie Small and Fernando Sabino in "Silence" at the Richmond Ballet Studio Theatre, 2009.

hired Stoner Winslett to provide artistic direction. And the third came in 1983, when the first graduating class of ballet students inspired the troupe to turn professional, thereby helping to keep the best and brightest young performers right here in Richmond.

Though our Ballet may be best known for cherished holiday traditions like "The Nutcracker," its repertoire is not at all static. With each new set of dancers and performances comes a new sensibility, a new twist. And the Ballet does not simply offer credible versions of works of enduring value. It has also shifted toward significant works by choreographers of our own time, and perhaps even more actively, to entirely new works.

Our Ballet abides by a mission to "awaken and uplift the human spirit, both for audiences and artists…." This mission is no more compelling than in the *Minds in Motion* initiative, which is now entering its fifteenth year. Minds in Motion takes the Ballet into almost twenty area classrooms for a year-long program that teaches fourth graders

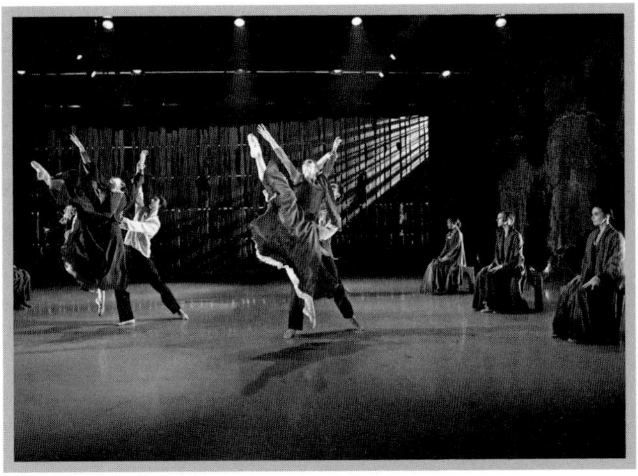

Richmond Ballet company members in "Misa Criolla," 2008. Feature performers pictured here are Shira Lanyi and Kirk Henning (center) and Angela Hutto and Thomas Garrett (left). "Misa Criolla" is scheduled for NYC's Joyce Theater in April of 2010.

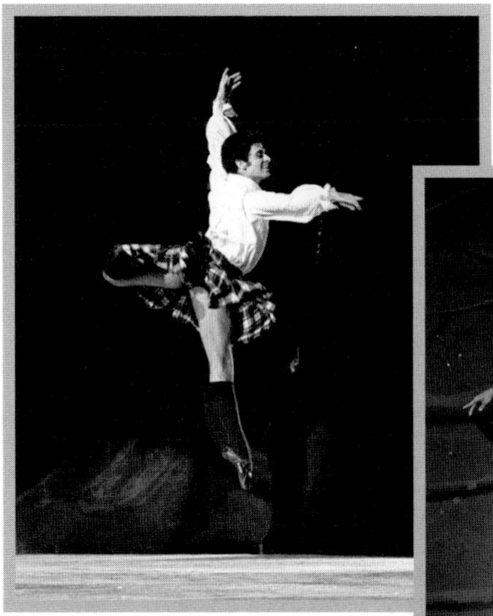

Fernando Bujones, guest artist in "La Sylphide", 1982. The ballet was still a volunteer ballet company.

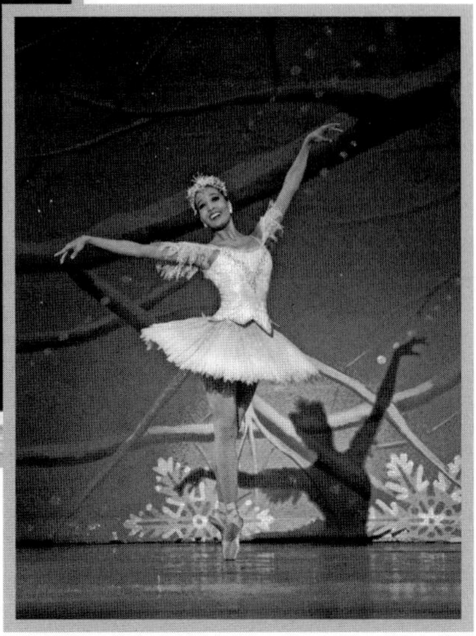

Maggie Small in "The Nutcracker" at the Landmark Theatre, 2008.

discipline, dedication, and self-awareness through dance. At the end of each program, all of the students – some 1,500 strong – join together on the stage of the Arthur Ashe Center to celebrate what they learned with their parents, loved ones, and friends far and near. These performances have brought audiences to tears, inspired them to hug strangers, or simply pause in their seats until the lights go out, marveling at all of the little creatures made tall through dance.

Our Ballet does not hang on a wall. It is a vital and transformative force in our community, serving apprentices, masters, students, and audiences of all sizes, shapes, colors, and ages. Just like an Aboriginal songline, our Ballet only comes alive through performance. And in the midst of one, the sheer, abiding, and creative genius of Stoner Winslett – our lady who shattered the glass slipper ceiling – is made real.

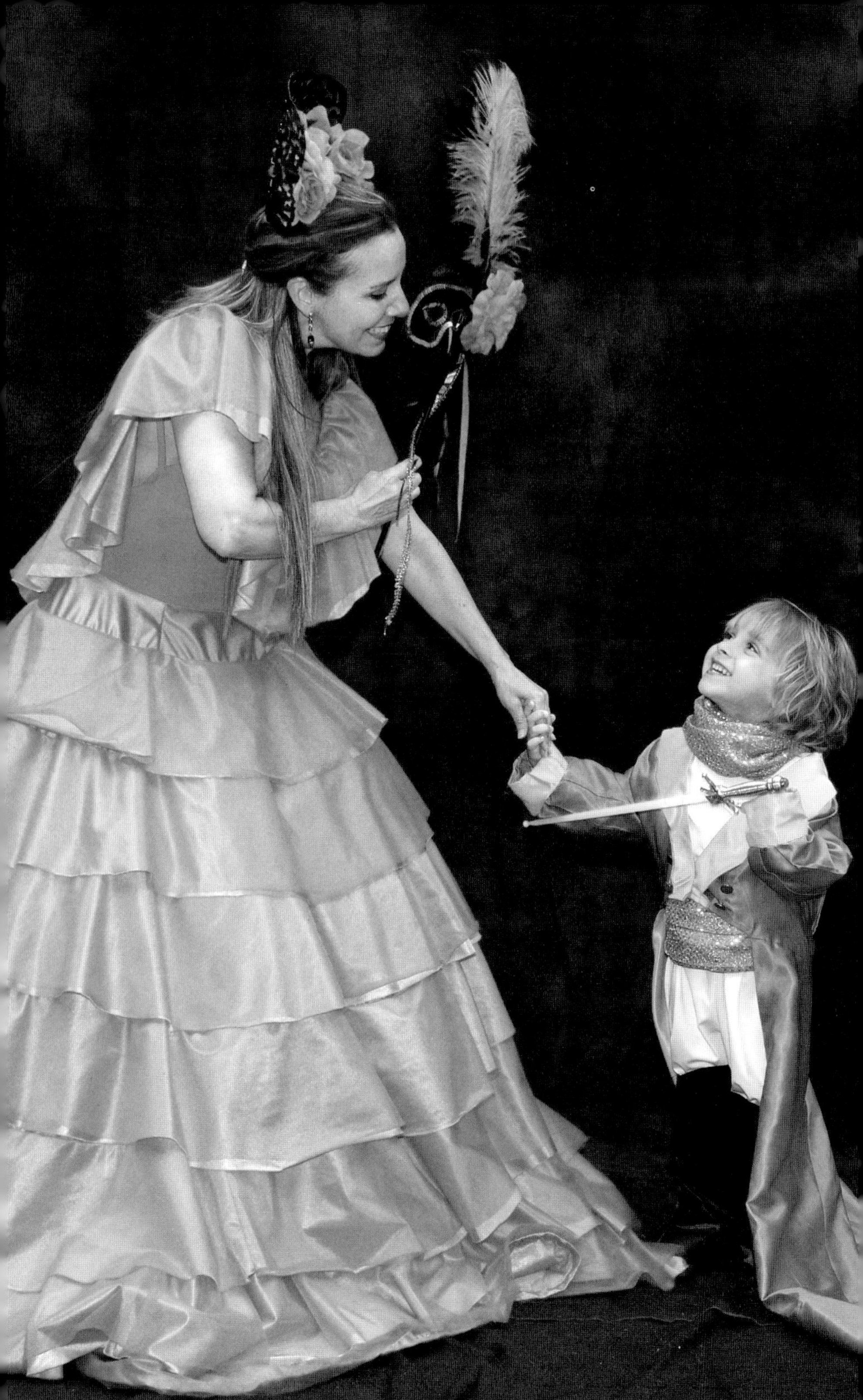

LATIN BALLET

Richmond has an enduring connection to Latin America. In the early 1800s, our trades of coffee in and flour out made Richmond one of the largest port cities in the United States. This commerce helped to steer local adventurers down into the wilds of the Andes. And it even inspired a "guano rush," as local farmers sought to revive their depleted soils by importing Peruvian bat dung. But despite a rich and irregular history with our southern neighbors, our most inspiring connection may be a contemporary one.

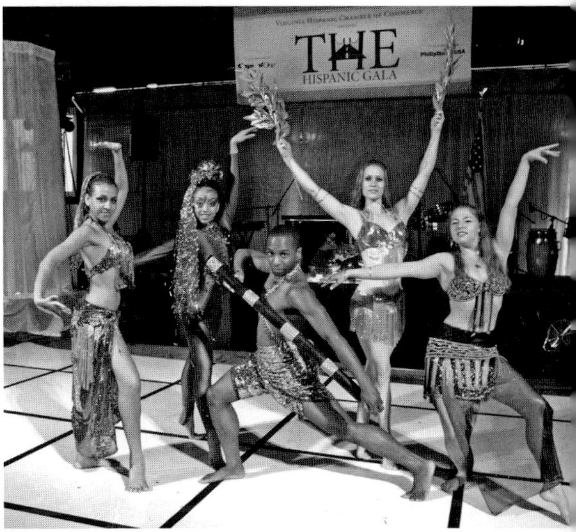

Members of the Latin Ballet performing at the Hispanic Chamber of Commerce Gala at the Science Museum, 2007.

In 1994, Ana Ines King followed "true love" from Columbia to Richmond. We now know Ana as the heart and soul of the Latin Ballet of Virginia, but back then, she was just a young dancer trying to find her way. Ana quickly became an ambassador of sorts, teaching Latin dance, history, and culture at VCU, as well as to second language students throughout the local public school system.

In 2000, Ana took her teaching to the center stage with a four-show production of "AmorAmerica" at the Glen Allen Cultural Arts Center.

◄ *Ana Ines King with an aspiring student, Daniela Nepstad, 2008.*

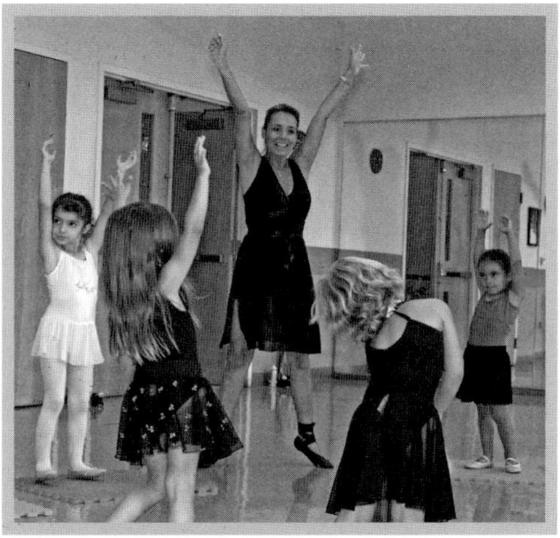

Ana Ines King with a group of her flamenco students at the Cultural Arts Center of Glen Allen, 2009.

The production was so successful that Ana was asked to do more, and more, and more. She was also invited to take her troupe to Columbia to perform at the Taetro Heredia, one of the oldest and most beautiful stages in the new world. Shortly after this adventure, Ana launched Richmond's first professional Latin ballet. And the rest, as they say, is history.

Ana's professional and junior companies are now preeminent in Virginia and beyond. But it is not simply the passion of their performance that distinguishes them. It is their absolute and unyielding commitment to preserve and promote Latin culture through an appreciation of all cultures. Among their 450 students are Russians and Chinese, Chileans and Argentineans, blacks and whites, little boys suffering from disabilities, and little girls recovering from abuse. Their youngest student is barely two and a half. Their oldest is ninety. And for all of them, whether through rumba or flamenco, salsa or meringue, a simple meditation seems to emerge, a meditation that Ana has carried with her all the way from her early days in South America – *a passion for dance, the love for life.*

Ana dreams only big dreams. She wants to nurture, protect, and empower those in her care. She wants to fill the stage with bodies in motion, bodies bent to songlines that reach deep into the old world. And she wants every one of us, whether young or old, fast-footed or slow, to join her. After all, as Ana likes to say, "If you can walk, you can dance."

Out Latin connection is not what it once was. It is better, richer, and more tantalizing, both to the eye and to the heart. And if we're lucky, we'll all enjoy a few more tangos before the curtain falls.

LATIN BALLET OF VIRGINIA

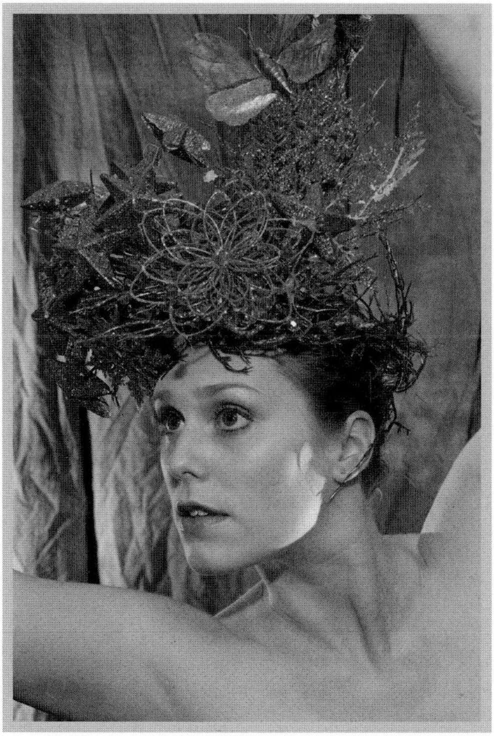

Lauren Davis as the North Star in the "Legend of the Poinsettia," 2009.

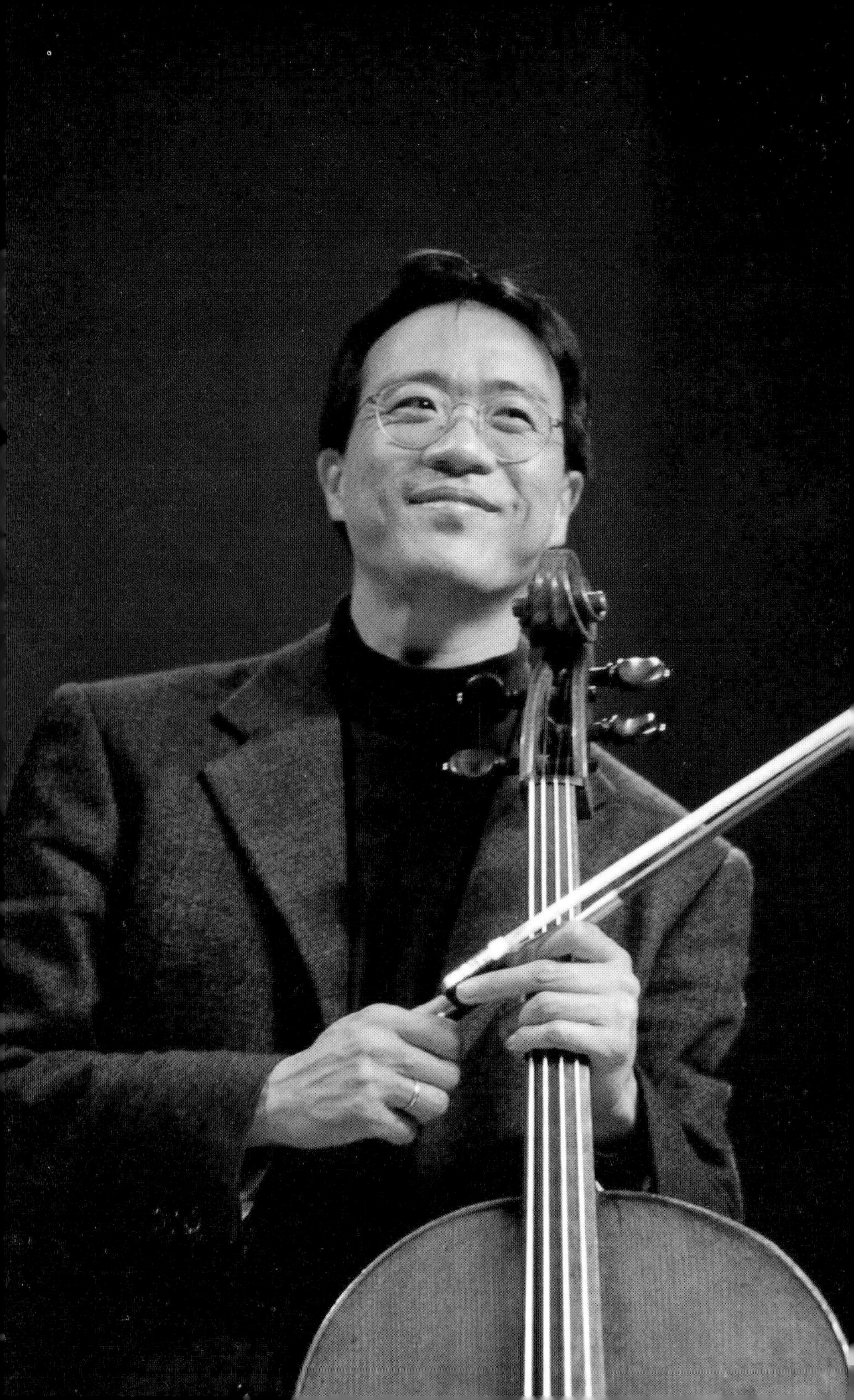

MODLIN CENTER

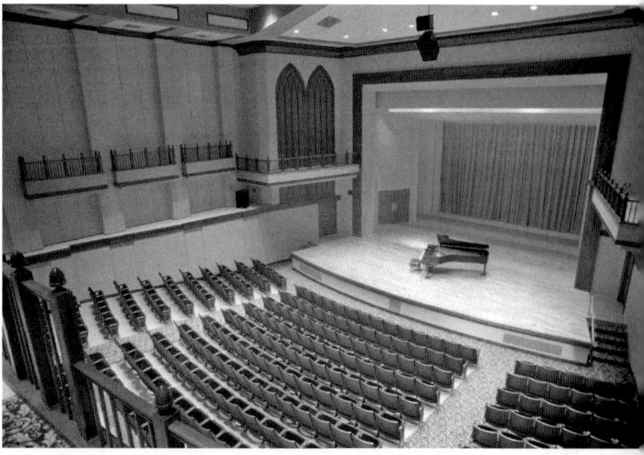
Camp Concert Hall, 1996.

For a school that traces its roots back to 1834, with distinctions in nearly every discipline, it is hard to imagine any pang of unfulfilled expectation. But that was precisely the feeling that touched our venerable University of Richmond in the 1980s and early 90s. There was a sense that the arts needed to be restored to the liberal arts experience of both faculty and students. And though the arts had always been a foundational aspect of the University, some arts had suffered, at least for a time, from the dint of other priorities.

All of this changed upon the opening of the George M. Modlin Center for the Arts in October 1996. Named for the University's Emeritus Chancellor, and inspired by President Dick Morrill's vision of a vibrant arts village, the Modlin Center erupted onto the scene with an inaugural series that sought to inspire diversity onstage and off.

Though originally conceived as disciplinary diversity, the Modlin Center's great legacy has been a cultural one, both among the students and their community. Its early organizers sought the

◄ *Yo Yo Ma in a Modlin Center Concert at the Carpenter Center for the Performing Arts, February, 2000.*

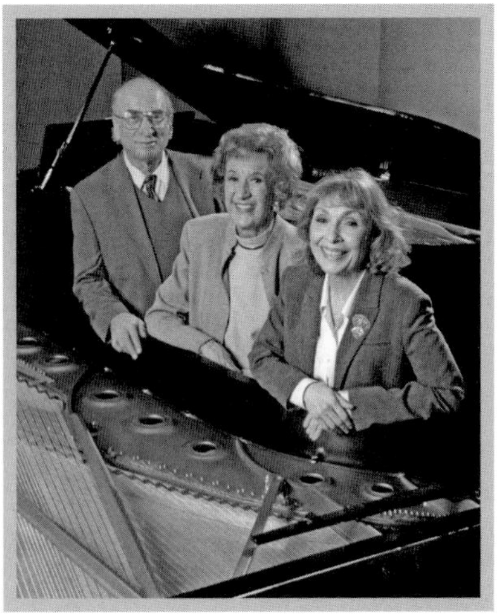

Dick Hyman, Mary McPartland and Ruth Laredo, performing as The Modlin Trio, in Three Piano Crossover, January, 2001.

freedom to be creative in challenging the appetites of their audiences. They brought us the Dance Theatre of Harlem, Celtic Roots, the Klesmer Conservatory Band, Lakota Dancers, Ladysmith Black Mambazo, and Yo-Yo Ma. And they created over twenty merit scholarships to help recruit bright young artists into the University. They also sought to drive programming toward the furthest reaches of academic research into ethno-musicology.

The City of Richmond, of course, is neither anchored nor necessarily swayed by what happens up on Westhampton Way. It is home to several preeminent institutions of higher learning, and to both professional and near-professional troupes of every artistic discipline. The Modlin Center's early organizers respected this, and sought to engage the larger community in a way that was good for everyone. They partnered with the Carpenter Center, Virginia Commonwealth University,

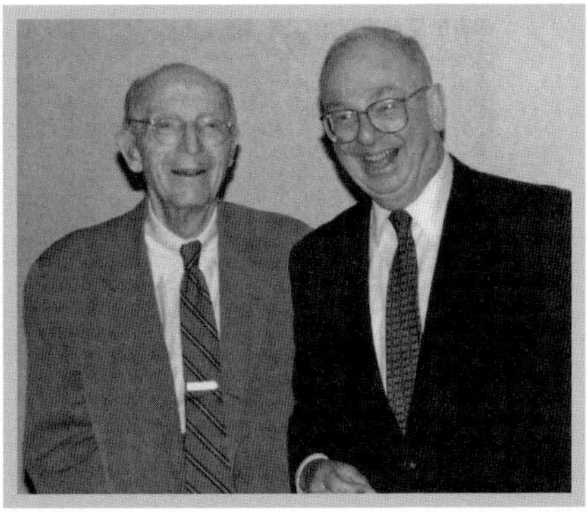

Dr. George M. Modlin, for whom the Modlin Center was named, and Lewis T. Booker, for whose family the Booker Hall of Music was named.

and others to help invigorate the City's cultural landscape. And they continue these partnerships today.

Nothing lasts forever. This year, the Modlin Center will bid an appreciative farewell to its first artistic director and prepare for a second one. It will reshuffle the raw materials of stage, studio, library, and lab and surely emerge with something different, a new vision, a different sensibility. But the Modlin Center will never lose the transformational roots that helped it to grow from unfulfilled to great expectation. And it will abide in its mission to celebrate every form of artistic endeavor on campus and off.

President Morrill is affectionately known as the Dali Lama of the Modlin Center. And the entire arts village of Richmond is richer for his vision.

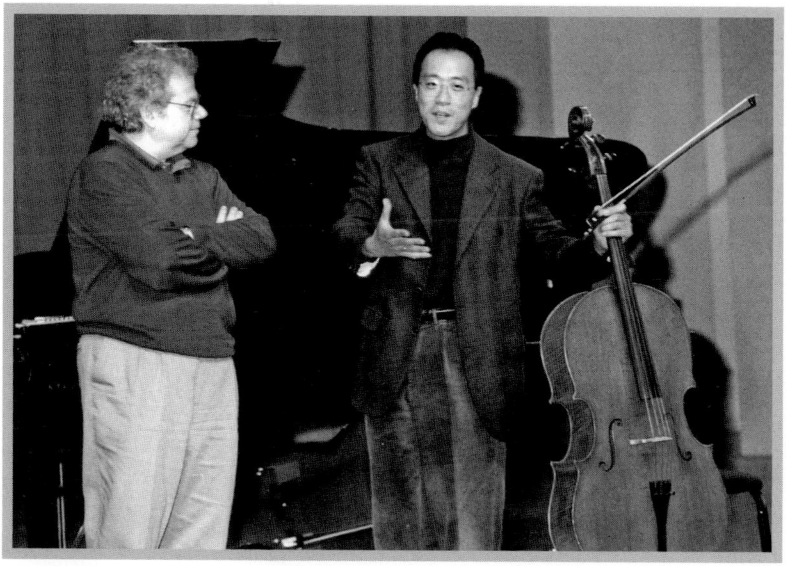

Emanuel Ax &Yo Yo Ma in a master class at Camp Concert Hall, 2000.

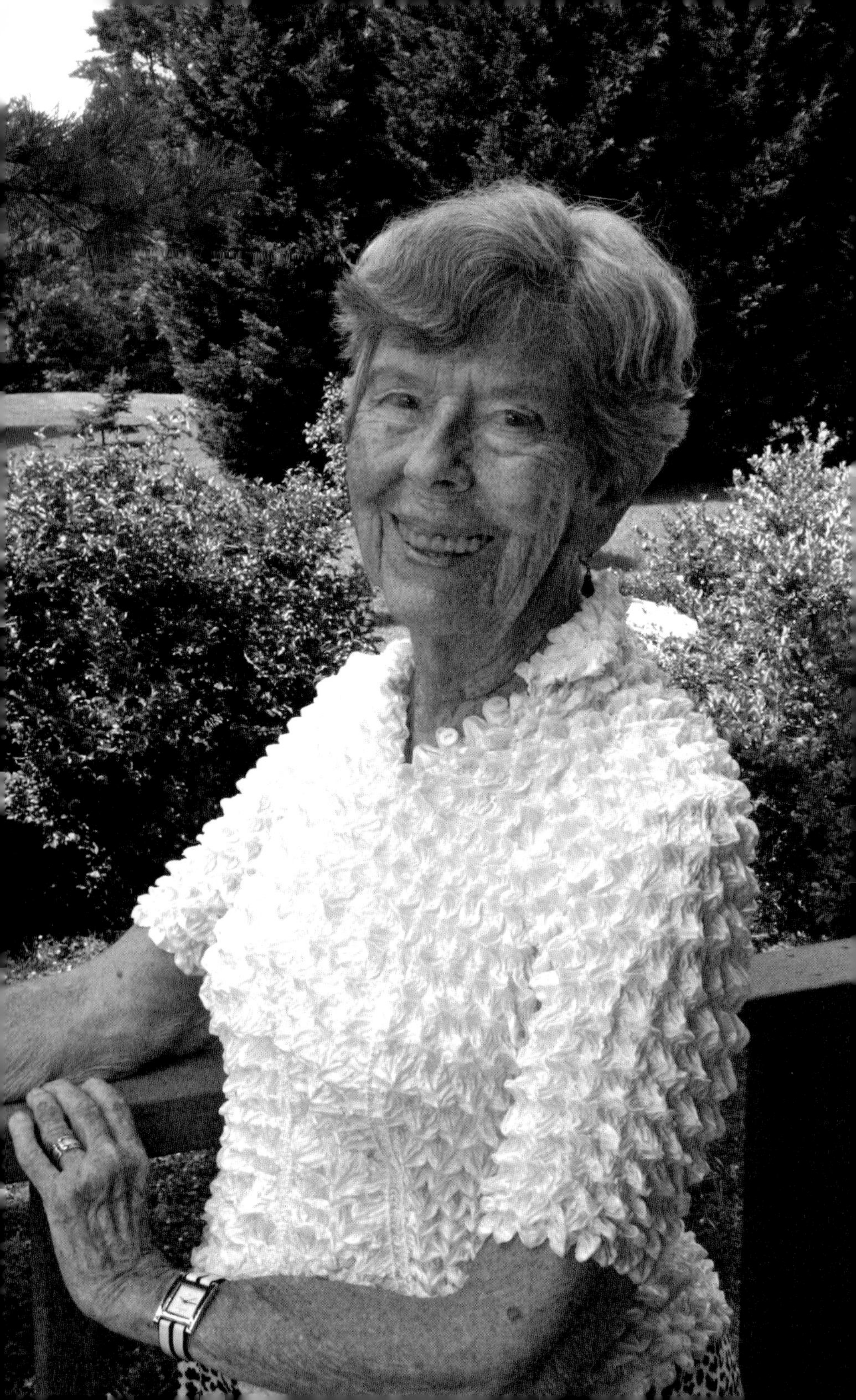

VCU Dance

We tend to measure the power of a university in terms of bricks and mortar – in a school's capacity to provide both space and place for students to learn. But the real power of a university is its ability to inspire and transform. And this, of course, takes more than bricks and mortar. It takes teachers willing to grow gray in the unrelenting pursuit of academic excellence, creativity, and those fleeting "ah ha" moments that young minds sometimes experience when they stumble upon some central unifying principle in algebra, French, and art, or other seemingly disconnected fields of study.

Virginia Commonwealth University may be best known these days for the physical transformation of its campuses along Broad, Belvidere, and downtown, and for the infusion of beautiful new sightlines into the City's skyline. But the school is so much more than bricks and mortar. VCU boasts one of the premier arts schools in the country, with over 3,000 students in sixteen arts-oriented departments. The school owes this distinction to its formative educators: Theresa Pollak, the nationally recognized painter, who started the arts department back in 1928; Raymond Hodges, the magician of stage craft, who

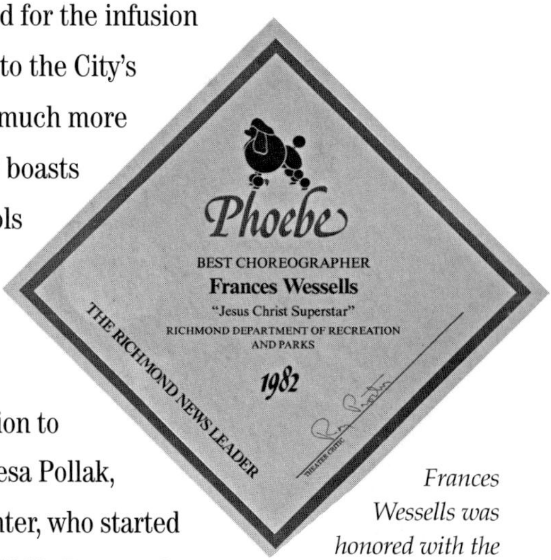

Frances Wessells was honored with the Phoebe Award for her performance in Jesus Christ Superstar, 1982.

◄ *Frances Wessells at her Goochland home, 2009.*

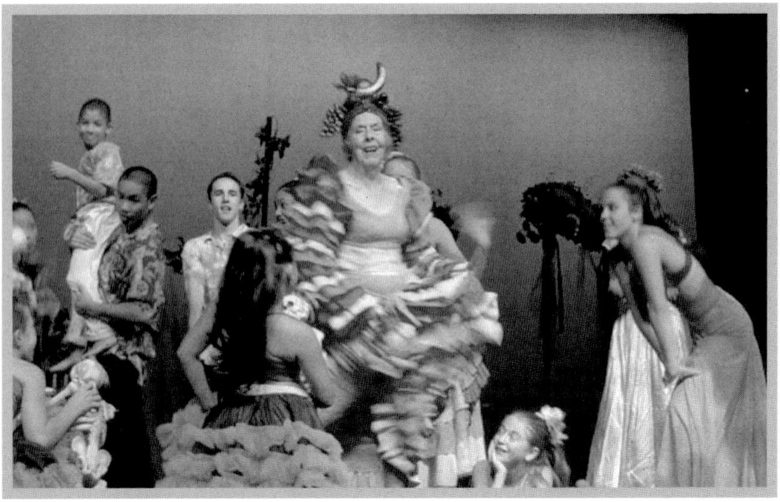

Frances Wessells as Carmine Miranda, 2006.

started the theatre department in 1942; and Frances Wessells, the maestra of modern dance, who started the dance department in 1981. Each deserves a full-blown biography, but in this little space, Frances holds special sway.

Frances Wessells is 90 years old. She has been teaching dance since 1942. She spent three years at Sweet Briar, twenty-five years at the University of Richmond, and another thirty (and counting) at VCU. Together with Dean Murry DePillars, Frances helped to pry dance loose from VCU's Health and Physical Education Department and establish it as a stand-alone department within the School of the Arts. VCU Dance is now preeminent, fostering not just artistic excellence but an environment of communication, mutual respect, and self-motivation among its students.

Over her career, Frances has studied with the best, including Hanya Holm, one of the four originators of the modern dance movement. She has also taught the best, including Chris Burnside, who later went on to chair VCU's Department of Dance and Choreography. Frances has inspired literally thousands of dancers through her own performances, compositions, and teaching. But she seems to be motivated by neither fame, nor fortune, nor personal legacy. Rather, Frances is motivated by a simple and abiding love of dance. As she likes to reflect, "All my life, I've known I had to do it. It didn't matter where or how, just so long as I could."

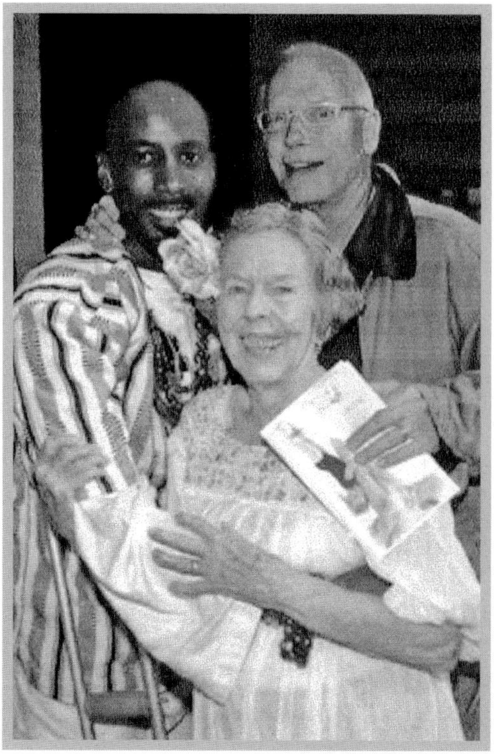

Frances Wessells, with fellow performer Monteleake Jones, and former VCU Dance Department Chairman, Chris Burnside, celebrate a successful performance.

Frances' love for dance is infectious, so much so that even an inveterate flat-foot like me is inspired to give it a try. And that, I think, is her "ah ha" power. Among the bricks and mortar of the University's beautiful new sightlines, at least a few should be marked in tribute to Frances Wessells, the heart and soul of VCU Dance.

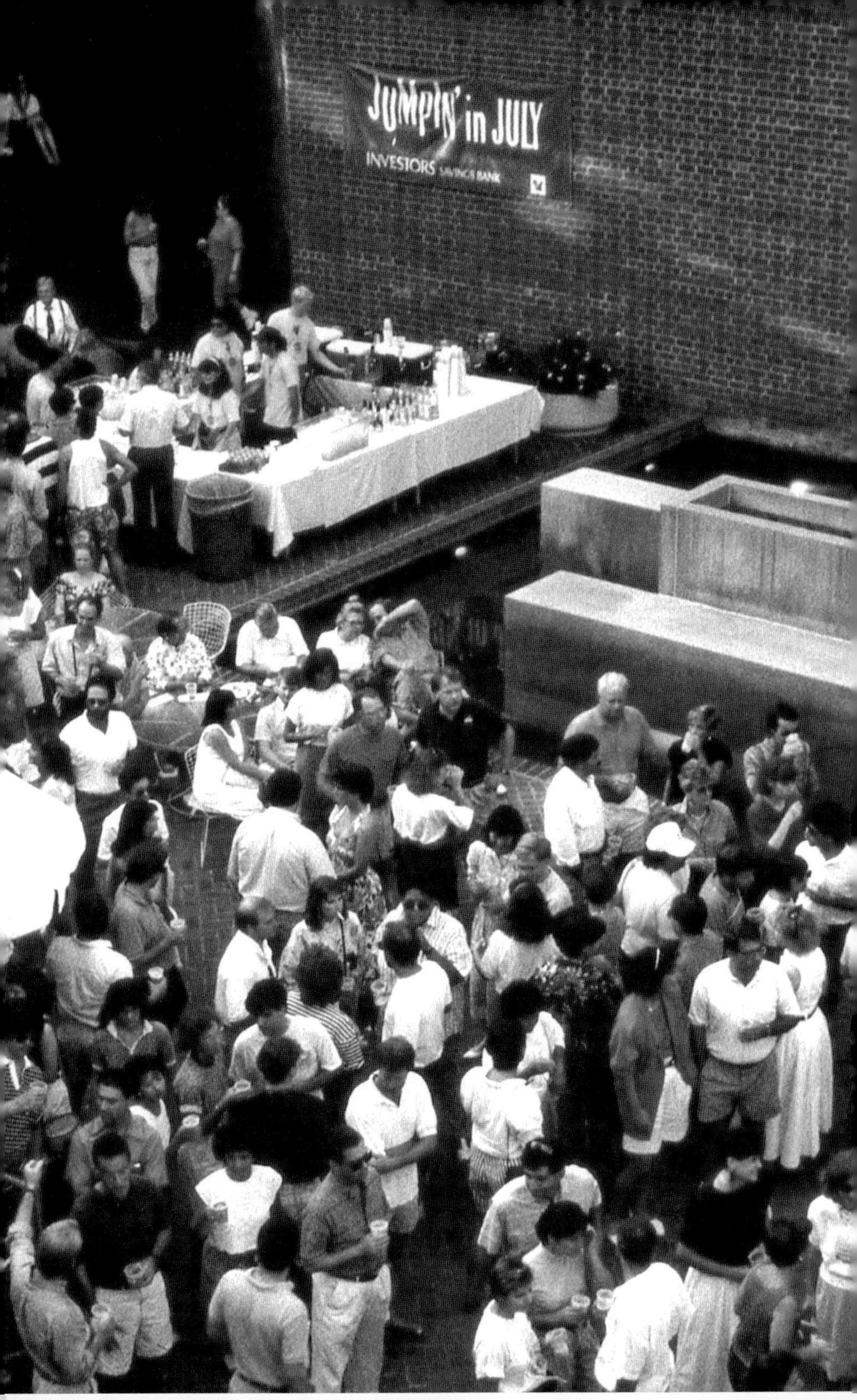
JUMPIN' in JULY
INVESTORS SAVINGS BANK

Dynamic Arts at VMFA

Change is the wellspring of our City. It lurks in the roiling waters of the mighty James, in our streetscape and skyline, even in the hues of color and contrast that mark the storylines of our little metropolis. And every so often, change even sneaks into the most enduring of our institutions.

The Virginia Museum of Fine Arts is my Muse. She is a place of contemplation and quietude amidst the gilded frames and stone statues of old masters. But, to my happy surprise, she is also a place of experiment and change.

The first big change came in 1955 when the museum opened a grand new theatre in an attempt to better integrate the fixed arts with the dynamic ones. At the time, the museum was considered to be a "pioneer" – the first in the country to promote performing arts as part of an overall museum program. The potential was profound.

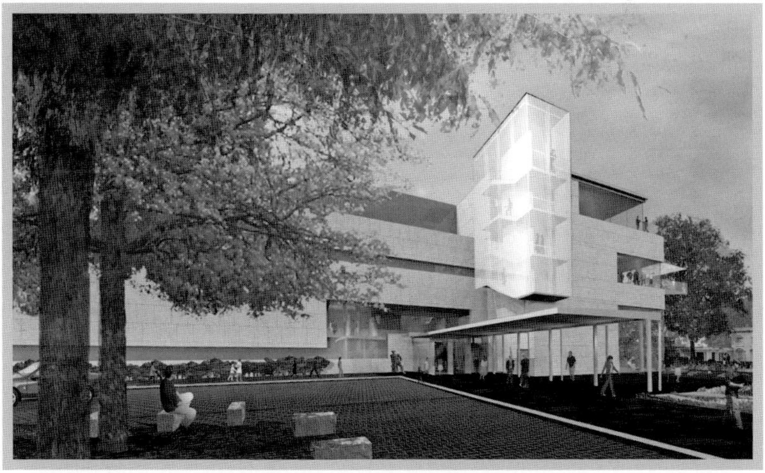

Architect's Rendering of the Virginia Museum of Fine Arts, scheduled to reopen in May, 2010.

◄ *Jumpin' in July, July 28, 1988.*

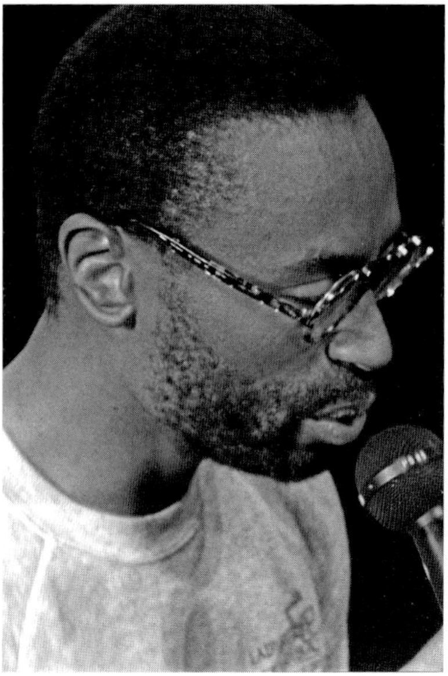
Bobby McFerrin at Fast Forward, 1988.

Just imagine enticing a visitor to the 18th century collection of paintings upstairs, and then to an 18th century drama downstairs. Imagine drawing noisy thespians into the quietude, or hermetic artists into the noisy fray of the stage. It was, as founder Leslie Cheek Jr. liked to say, a "noble experiment."

The second big change came thirty years later when the museum opened its new west wing. Coupled with its emerging focus on modern art, the museum launched an experimental performing arts program designed to "fast forward" audiences to a new age of music and dance. The inaugural series featured performances by Philip Glass, Steve Reich, and other composers of this new age. Captivating to some and just plain noise to others, perhaps the greatest challenge in these performances was finding words to describe them. The newspaper tried its best, using phrases like "disassociated ecstasy," "propulsive dynamism," "sonic sparsity," and "heavy metal classical." But I think that when trying to describe the brainwaves of a dream turned inside out, one is best served by simply making up an entirely new word, let's say, haroowa!

This haroowa galvanized public attention, and the "fast forward" series went on to great distinction with headline-grabbing performances by the legendary modern dance choreographer, Merce Cunningham, as well as the vocal gyroscope, Bobby McFerrin. But realizing that the new age of music might not be accessible to everyone, the museum also launched a more laid-back, "normal age" series called Jumpin' in July. Jumpin' changed the face of the sculpture garden, from an austere walk-about to a packed stage where beer flowed liberally, pretty people cavorted, and music rocked long into the night – past the curfew of the princes and princesses in their gilded frames inside, and under the quizzical eye of the normally severe, hermit saint in Luca Giordano's masterpiece.

The galleries have just gone dark as the museum finishes a massive expansion that will open to the world in 2010. Whatever ends up back on the walls, one thing is certain. Experiment and change will continue to be the wellspring of the museum, and through it, our fair City.

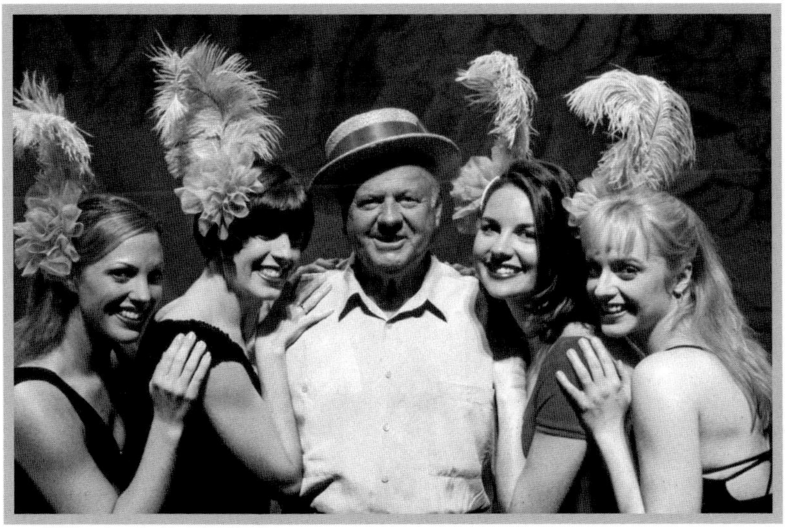

Dick Van Patton in "Scandals," at Theatre Virginia.

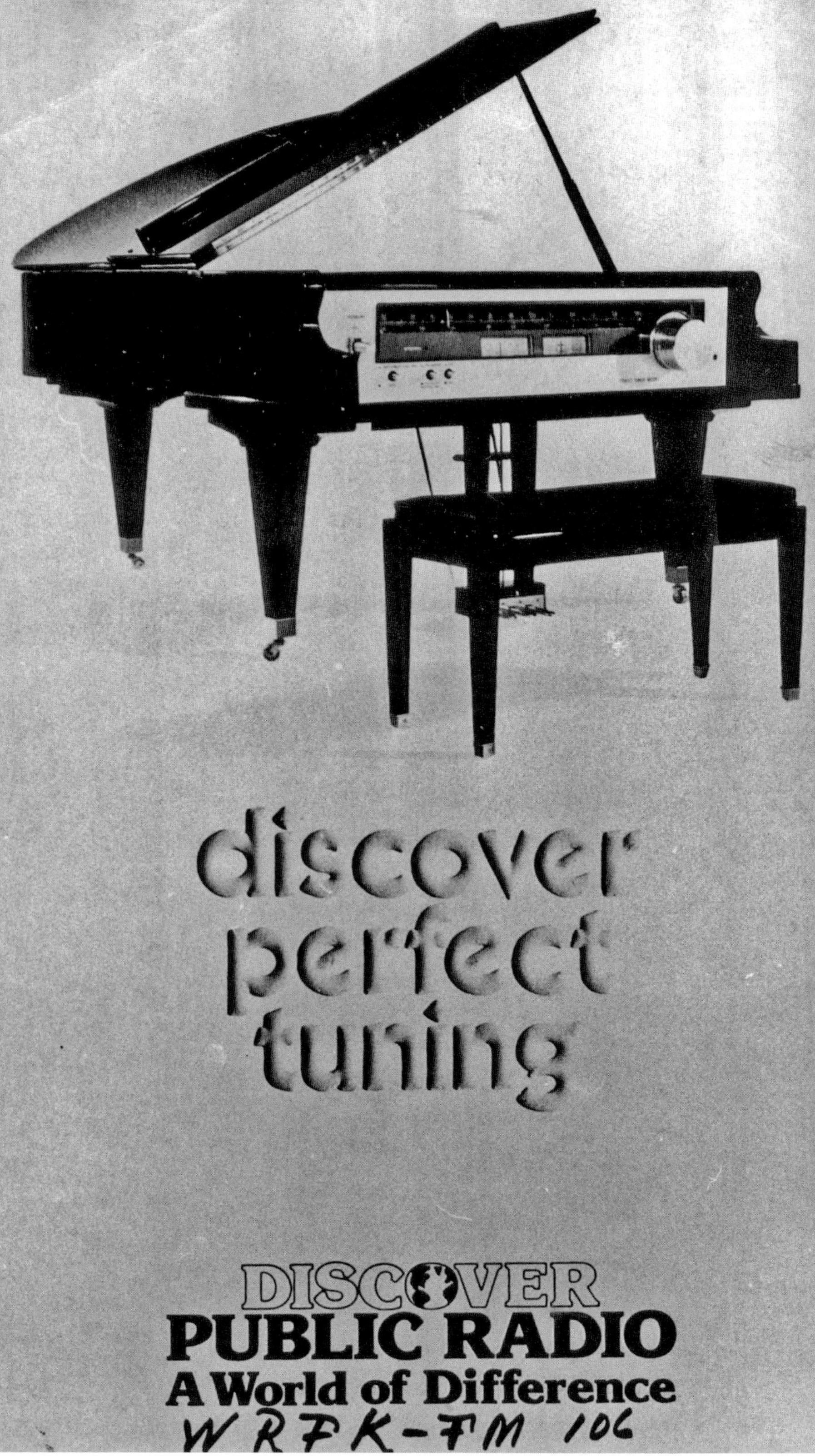
discover
perfect
tuning
DISCOVER
PUBLIC RADIO
A World of Difference
WRFK-FM 106

ROOTS OF PUBLIC RADIO

WCVE Public Radio is a trusted friend, a confidant, nearly family. It is a voice of calm in times of distress; a voice of reason and much-needed humor. Day or night, WCVE Public Radio is there for us with music, news, and perspective – all of it thought-provoking and respectful. It brings the world into our homes. And every once in a while, it impels us to pause in our tracks for those sparks of inspiration, or incredulity, or incalculable sorrow known as "driveway moments."

WCVE Public Radio is our portal to NPR, the brain-child of an unexpectedly lucid Congress, which in 1967 declared that public broadcasting would further our general welfare and constitute an expression of diversity and excellence for all of the citizens of our Nation. Not just that, but more. That it was in the public interest to encourage the development of programming that involved creative risks and that addressed the needs of unserved and underserved audiences, particularly children and minorities.

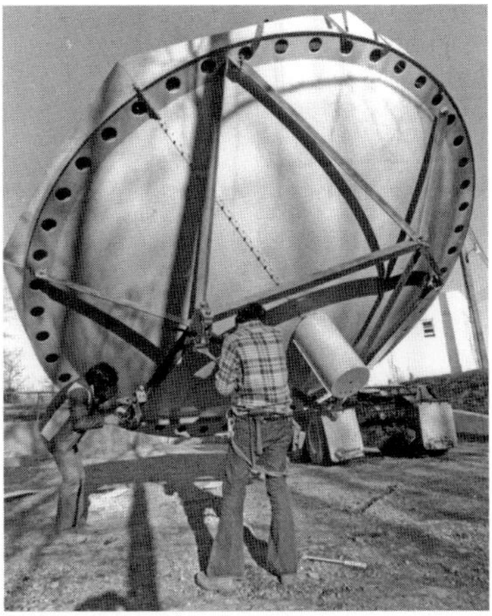

Juan Castelanos and David Dompeling work on satellite dish, 1979.

When President Johnson signed the Public Broadcasting Act into law on November 7, 1967, he remarked that "our Nation wants more than just material wealth; our Nation wants more than a 'chicken in every pot.' We in America have an appetite for excellence, too.

◄ *WRFK Poster, 1980.*

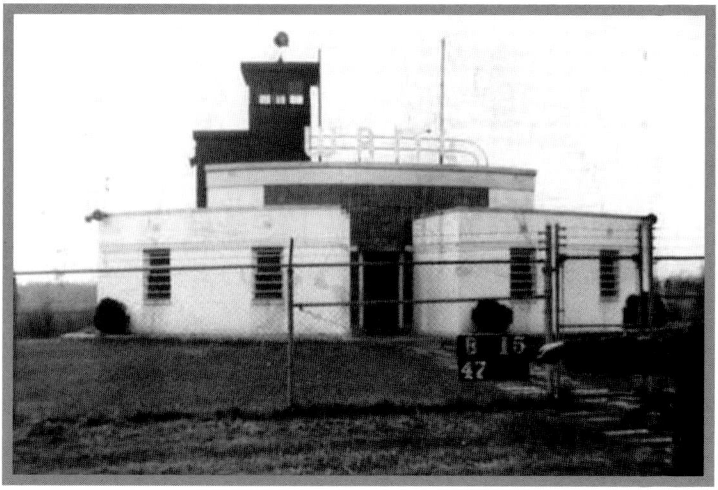

Original WRFK Building.

While we work every day to produce new goods and to create new wealth, we want most of all to enrich man's spirit." And that, he said, "is the purpose of this act."

But public radio in Richmond was already an emergent force by 1967. Our very own WRFK 106 FM had been broadcasting from Union Theological Seminary since May 27, 1957. And when NPR eventually formed in 1970, WRFK was one of the first charter members in the country.

This is not to say that our public broadcasting experiment has always been free from doubt. In fact, in 1988, we almost lost public radio in Richmond for good. But thanks to the sustained effort of loyal listeners and Central Virginia Educational Television, we only lost it for two minutes. At 1:28 p.m. on May 6, 1988, WRFK went off the air. At 1:30 p.m., WCVE signed on. Its first broadcast was Aaron Copeland's *Fanfare for the Common Man.* And as its first operations manager was proud to say, "[WCVE] is dedicated to the people, who will be our voice and guide."

The station moved from its temporary home at 101.1 to 88.9 FM in October 1989, and we've found it there ever since. Sometimes, it's hard to be thankful unless you have a chicken in your own pot, or until you know the full measure of what you almost lost.

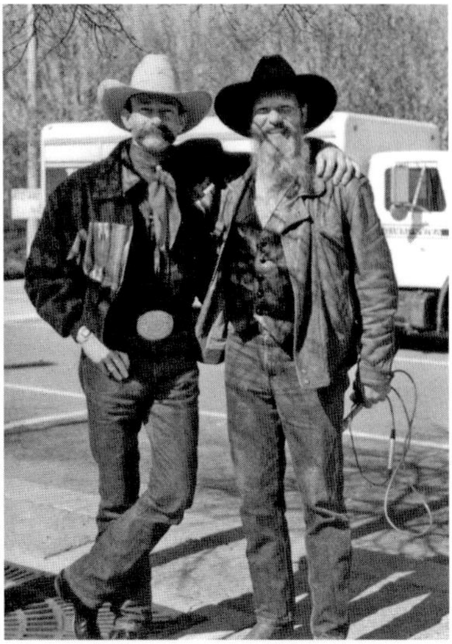

Baxter Black, Cowboy and Humorist, and Steve Clark, WCVE Producer.

If this is so, then let us never forget that two minute pause, or the joyful noise that followed. WCVE, this one's for you!

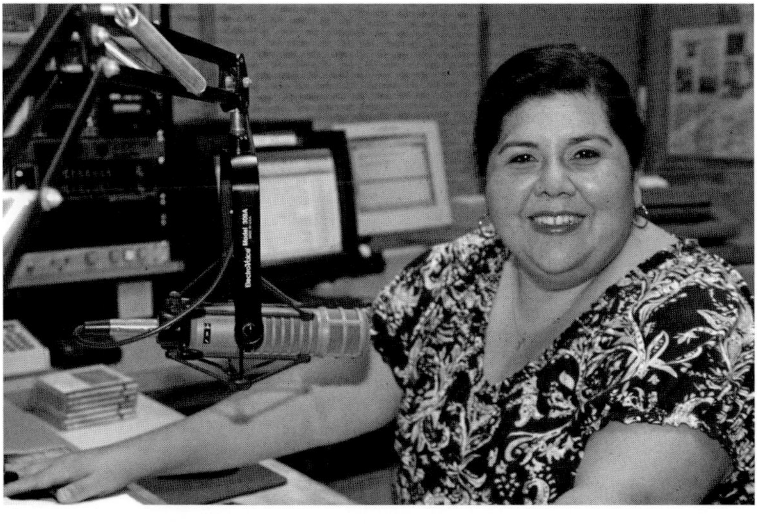

Bobbie Barajas, broadcasting her program, Classical Music with Bobbie Barajas, in the FM broadcasting studio.

AFTERWORD

In Richmond, there is a dear, old legend about the Bumtowners of Scuffletown, a not-so-terrifying gang of boys who would liberate all of the ash barrels in the Fan District to fuel a bonfire on Park Avenue – a bonfire that would burn bright from Halloween straight through to New Year's Day. As the legend goes, the neighboring homeowners tolerated the loss of their barrels because the boys promised security in exchange for a "see nothing, hear nothing" policy. And perhaps also, because the fire breathed strange beauty into the void.

This little book has only liberated a few of the barrels of old stories about performing arts, artists, and stages in our fair City. But we hope that they will burn bright, and perhaps one day, inspire more.

There are so many left to tell – stories about Shakespeare at Agecroft; Gwar on Grace; the old Mozart Academy of Music on Broad; jazz and blues and rock-and-roll; choir music so sweet that it will make you cry; the time that Bruce Springsteen played a concept on top of the 7th Street parking deck; the flophouse for wandering musicians

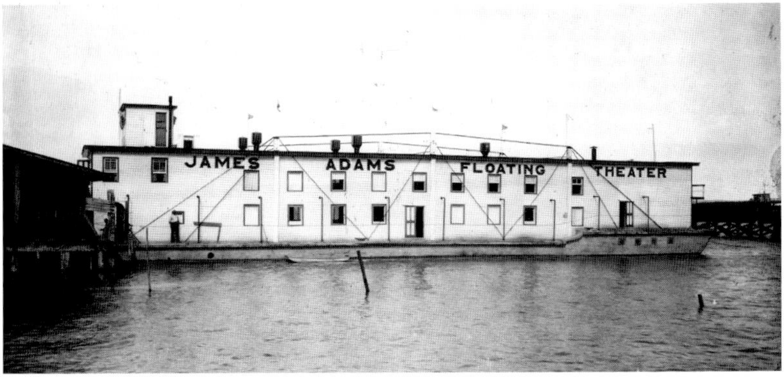

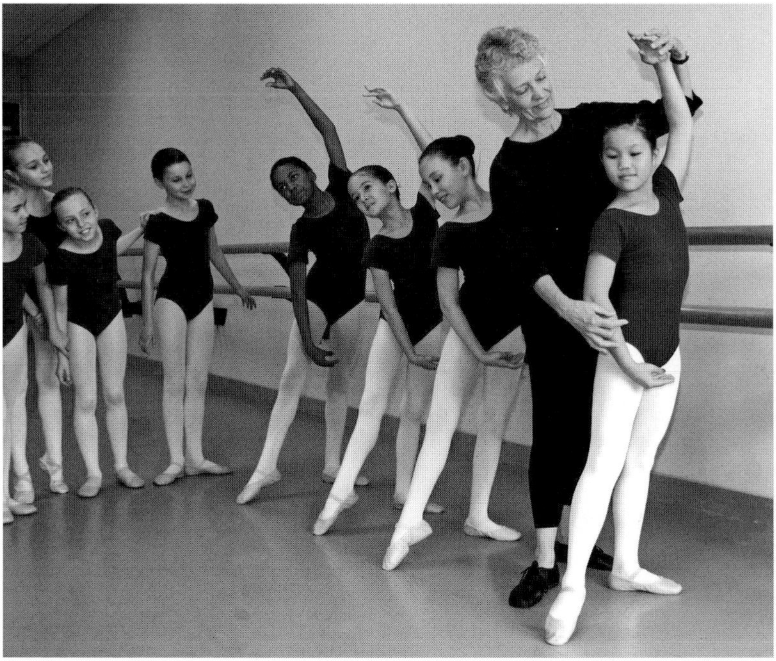

back in the 70s that surely rivaled the one in Cannery Row; a "floating theater" on the James River back in the 30s; the virtuoso violinist, Sy Gilliat, who was considered part of the "black aristocracy" in the early 1800s; Joe Jefferson, who literally became Rip Van Winkle while managing the old Marshall Theatre at 7th and Broad; and even the old crooners who sit on lonely street corners or the young kids who beat out their symphonies on upturned pails.

Remember, "songlines" is not a real word, and a song will not save us from starvation. But the lilting chords of a human voice do breathe strange beauty into the void, and maybe, just maybe, they will light our way home.

ACKNOWLEDGEMENTS

This book features stories that were developed with special research assistance from the Library of Virginia, Richmond Public Library, Valentine Richmond History Center, and Virginia Historical Society. It also features creative design details, photographs and other images provided courtesy of the following individuals and organizations:

1708 Gallery
Al Wertheimer
Black History Museum
Dianne Dementi
Ed Trask
Frances Wessells
Harvey Hudson
Jayne Hushen
Jennifer Smith
Jimmy and Donna Dean
Kathy Albers
Latin Ballet of Virginia
Richmond Ballet
Richmond CenterStage
Richmond Jazz Society
Richmond Times-Dispatch
Robbin Thompson
Shirley MacLaine
Steve Bassett
Suzanne Grandis
Theatre IV
The National
University of Richmond
Valentine Richmond History Center
VentureRichmond
Virginia Historical Society
Virginia Museum of Fine Arts
WCVE Public Radio
Wendy Addison
Whitaker Studio

We owe deep gratitude to all of the performing artists and arts organizations of our fair City. Without them, we would suffer far more than the loss of this little book.

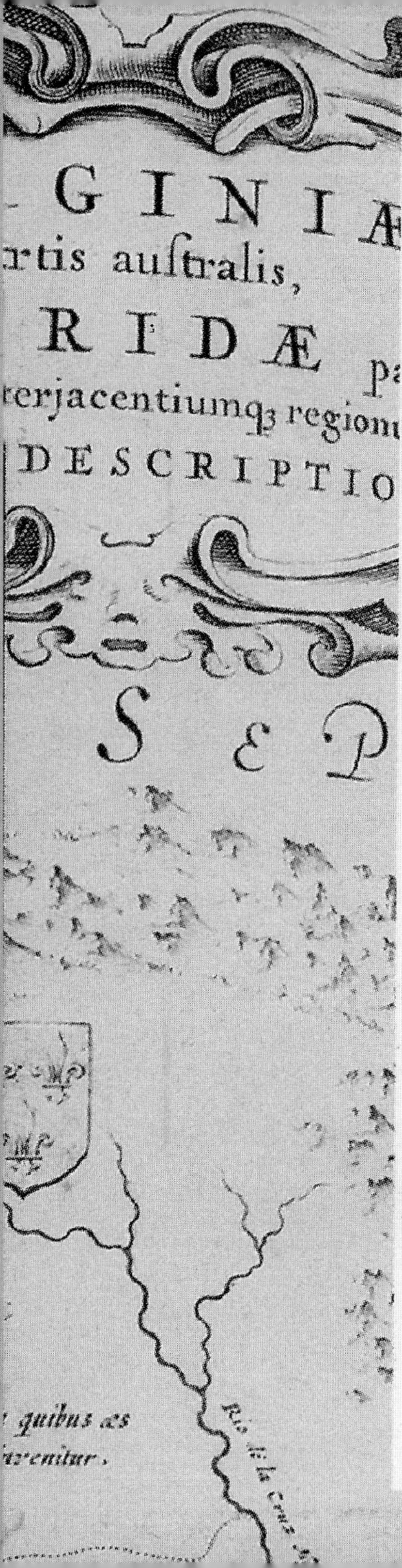

Donna and

"VIRO

From the Blue Ridge t
There's a commonwealt
As the mother of th
Heaven chose her as t
Virginia, de
There's no place c
Virginia, sw
My old Dominion h

When I think about
I remember dogwood
When the sun sets or
Sometimes, I think
They sing Virgin
There's no place c
Virginia, sw
My old Dominion h
My old Dominion h

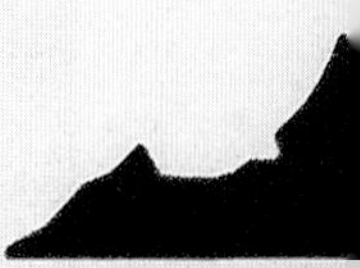